Joyce at Last
and Other
Short Plays

Michael G. Casey

ISBN 978-1-9160264-7-6

First edition, 2020

Published by Azimuth Publishing
Dublin, Ireland

Cover painting of Joyce: Peter FitzGerald / iCulture

This version of *Joyce at Last and Other Short Plays* uses greyscale
images; a full-colour version is also available through Amazon.

Layout, cover design by iCulture

Please visit michaelgcasey.com

BOOKS PREVIOUSLY PUBLISHED BY MICHAEL G. CASEY

Come Home, Robbie, a novel, published by The O'Brien Press, 1990

> "…page-turning urgency … spine-tingling compulsion … the sheer quality of the writing lends the story some of the stature of heroic tragedy."
> —The Education Times

Treadmill, an award-winning Chapbook of short stories, published by Tipperary Arts Centre and Start Magazine, 2008

> "…Casey brings to life vivid characters who captivate, amuse and engage … (He) has a wry observation and quick wit."
> —Mike McCormack

Ireland's Malaise: The Troubled Personality of the Irish Economy, published by The Liffey Press, 2010

> "…(Casey) shows the same Confucian wisdom as his hero, T.K. Whitaker in his brilliant new book."
> —Eoghan Harris, The Sunday Independent

The Visit, a novel, published by The Anaphora Press, 2011

Broken Circle, a collection of poetry, due to be published by Salmon Press in Spring 2020

Michael G. Casey's most recent novels are *Smudged Mascara*, *Maura's Dance with Uncle Sam*, *The Killing of Ros Grenham*, *Proving Ground* and *Divers Kinds*. Those books, plus *Joyce's Wake*, a Book of *Full-length Plays*, are all from Azimuth Publishing. They are available in Kindle and print versions through Amazon.

INTRODUCTION

As in the first volume of plays, I wish to thank the Umbrella Theatre Company for producing many of the plays contained in this second volume, in particular Gerard Dalton, Celia de Fréine and Michael O'Meara. Gratitude is due to the Henrik Ibsen Museum for putting on Joyce at Last in Oslo. This was highly appropriate since Joyce was such a great admirer of Ibsen's work and, according to some authorities, taught himself Norwegian to understand it better.

Many of the plays were inspired by paintings in the National Gallery of Ireland and were performed in one of the public spaces of that institution. At some stage during the performance of each play the painting in question was projected onto a screen on stage. The audiences were impressed by the combination of the dramatic and the purely visual – and many, indeed, wondered why this kind of fusion had not been done before.

Many actors gave their time and talent willingly, and to them I am deeply indebted. They include:

Martin Brennan, Brid Turner, Rosemary Keogh, Ian Condron, Ann Kennedy, Pat O'Grady, Joan Fleetwood, Mark Colreavy, Michael Heavey, Val O'Donnell, Ian Blackmore, Denise O'Connor, Sarah Coughlin, Maeve Delargy, Mike Timms,

Denise O'Connor, James Daniel Murphy, Roy Grimson, Dick Tobin, Mark Aylward, and Louis O'Byrne.

Many of these actors were also writers and directors, and were involved in other theatre companies, e.g. the Dublin Shakespeare Society. Without the intelligent feedback they provided during rehearsals, the productions would have been very much poorer. On a personal note, I always keenly observed the read-throughs of my plays, noting when an actor seemed to have difficulty with a line. This usually indicated a problem, e.g. the line in question was 'out of character'. It might have been a good line, taken in isolation, but it just didn't fit and, therefore had to be dropped. I depended to a large extent on the visceral reaction of actors who, it must be remembered, inhabit the parts they play. Their instincts have to be taken seriously.

The plays in this volume are in no particular order except that the more serious ones are presented first, i.e., the first seven plays. The ones following are more light-hearted though with a fair sprinkling of grey-to-black humour. It is hoped that none of them will give offence or appear to be politically incorrect. If we can't question taboos in the theatre (or universities), culture will be slower to develop and may, indeed, ossify.

"It is possibly the ekphrastic plays in this collection – those based on paintings in the National Gallery of Ireland – that are the key to why the texts here are so compelling. An idea, once sparked to life here, goes where its own logic takes it, to great effect."

—Peter FitzGerald

DEDICATION

For my mother

TABLE OF CONTENTS

JOYCE AT LAST

A One-Man Play

Flyer for the première of *Joyce at Last*, 2015; *front*

JOYCE At Last

Understanding the Man behind the Literature

Dlr Lexicon Studio, Dun Laoghaire

Saturday 11th & Sunday 12th June 2016 at 8pm

PRESENTED BY UMBRELLA THEATRE COMPANY

Produced and directed by Gerard Dalton

A must-see event at the start of the 2016 Dublin Bloomsday Festival.

JOYCE At last is a new short play by **Michael Casey**, which has been selected by the Norwegian Irish Society as the main theatrical event at the 7th Oslo Bloomsday Festival on 16th June 2016. The play is set in 1940. James Joyce reflects on his life, as he is about to depart on his final journey to Switzerland, weeks before his death.

Prior to its Oslo première, two special weekend performances will take place in the dlr Lexicon Studio on Saturday 11th and Sunday 12th June at 8pm.

This new theatrical piece, performed by **Martin Brennan** as James Joyce, will incorporate, for the Lexicon performances, images of Joyce's live and live music from the talented singer /songwriter, **Harry Kearns**, whose album **Before You Go** has just been released.

The second part of this unique programme will include a conversation with James Joyce's grandnephew, **Jurek Delimata** and playwright **Michael Casey**.

REVIEWS

JOYCE'S WAKE by Michael Casey

'Fantastic production. Wonderful writing and superb performances all round.'

'What a wonderful play. Script was terrific, clever and flowed beautifully.'

BEFORE YOU GO by Harry Kearns

'I've been working with a very talented songwriter by the name of Harry Kearns. Some might know him, many will not, but if there is any justice in this world you will know his music...Needless to say this could be a very big album if it finds its way into the right hands, so do try and get one of the first editions. Gareth Desmond, Loop Studios, Dublin.

OTHER UMBRELLA PRODUCTIONS TO LOOK OUT FOR IN 2016

KATIE & BETH by Lia Mills & Celia De Fréine - Mill Theatre, Dundrum, Monday 6th- Saturday 11th June 2016 at 1pm.

LUÍSE by Celia De Fréine. The story of Louise Gavan Duffy – Scoil Bhríde, Ranelagh, Thursday 15th – Saturday 17th September 2016.

LEGACY: from Patrick to Pearse - Eight new short plays inspired by historical paintings from the National Gallery collection, National Gallery of Ireland, Merrion Square , Saturday 15th October 2016 and other later dates.

 dlr

Contact: umbrellatheatrecompany@gmail.com

Flyer for the première of *Joyce at Last*, 2015; *back*

JAMES JOYCE *and his wife, Nora, have decided to leave Paris and go back to Zurich to avoid the Second World War. Their daughter, Lucia, who failed as an interpretative dancer, is in a mental hospital in German-occupied France; she will spend the rest of her life in an institution. Their son, Giorgio, has married Helen Kastor Fleischman, a wealthy American heiress ten years his senior. They and their two sons travel between Europe and New York. But the marriage is in difficulty. Giorgio has failed as a singer and is drinking heavily. Helen, who is highly strung, will also end up in a mental hospital.*

Now, towards the end of his life, and with all of his literary work behind him, JOYCE *reflects on the sad state of his family.*

He sits at a table with a bottle of white wine and a glass. His magnifying glass is also on the table and his cane rests against it. The family portrait hangs on a wall. Nearby, on the floor, is a suitcase half-filled with books and documents. He will soon be leaving Paris for Zurich to avoid the war. His sight is very bad – he is wearing an eye-patch – and he is suffering from stomach problems. He delivers the following monologue.

At the beginning of the monologue JOYCE, *though moved by the memory of his children as they were growing up, tends to make excuses for his poor parenting. He is quite objective about it and doesn't engage emotionally. But gradually, as he speaks and as he 'hears' snippets of dialogue in his head, he comes to realise more fully the nature of the damage done to his children. At the end he realises that he is largely to blame.*

(JOYCE, *standing, pours wine.*)
Thank God for Zurich and the neutral Swiss. I never thought we'd have to go there again to avoid a world war … a *second* one … yet go we must. Civilization, it seems, is no protection against war … It won't be easy to get out of occupied Paris … but that's another story…

Nora refuses to believe that I haven't much time left. Maybe she's trying to cheer me up. But I know what I know. This war will see me out … Stomach problems are the least of it. I've put my practical affairs in order, as they say…

(*He looks at the suitcase and sits.*)

… but I still have to deal with the more … emotional side of things … An examination of conscience as Catholics call it. Maybe order or structure doesn't apply to the heart. But I have to make sense of it all, or at least try. There won't be many more opportunities, probably none.

Nora threw down the gauntlet some weeks ago when she said that I had never been much good as a father or as a family man, that I had devoted all my energy to these two books…

(*He picks up Finnegans Wake and Ulysses.*)

"You didn't pay nearly enough attention to Lucia and Giorgio." That's what Nora said to me. It wasn't a barbed comment, and it wasn't given in anger – but there was something in her tone that pulled me up short. I may be smart and adept with words but Nora is wise; she has a great sense of the world, always had. It's in her blood. I learnt early on that it is foolish to ignore what she says.

(*He paces for a while and goes into defensive mode.*)

So, a bad father? Mmnnn … If this were a court scene the first and perhaps only witness I would call would be that old fart, Carl Jung. Why him? You might well ask.

He said I could dive into water and come up again. True in a way. *Total* immersion, nothing less for me. No half-measures … no dipping in a toe. Yes, I was happy, surrounded by water and snuffling in the sea-floor for alluvial deposits – little life-forms, microscopic cells. From them I could develop larger life-forms, characters with stories to tell. The Viennese chancer, Herr Doktor Freud, started his career by investigating the gonads of eels. A pity he didn't stay at it. Leave the deep-sea diving into the subconscious to the Bard and myself.

Speaking of the Bard, I've always believed that *Hamlet* was inspired by the death of Shakespeare's son, *Hamnet*. We can write well only about those who are near and dear.

(*He faces the audience.*)

I mean in 'Ulysses', I was both Bloom and Dedalus, and Nora was Molly. How else could I have put such passion and humanity into that book? How could I have coped with the sickening fear of adultery? Ulysses, Penelope and Telemachus had to be made real ... Every work of art is autobiographical at its heart, even if heavily disguised. But that's part of the problem: the emotional energy inspired by family is siphoned off into the printed word. Readers gain but families lose. That's how it is. There's only so much energy to go around.

(*He sits and drinks.*)

So, back to fatherhood and Nora's rebuke ... Well, *as* Jung implied, nothing else existed for me during those dives. Water clogged my ears. And my eyes were weak anyway, weak and blurred. I lived in a bubble that protected me for the work I had to do. My nose was firmly pressed into those handfuls of particles salvaged from the sea-floor.

(*He brings the books close to his face.*)

So, how could I concentrate on being a good parent? I was lost in another world, completely bound up in it. Did Nora understand that? I wonder.

Then there were dreams, fantasies and epiphanies – all of them absorbing in different ways. (*Pause*) So, that would be my main defence, thanks to Jung. I was a sponge, soaking up everything, squeezing it all out on paper, then diving into the sea again. That's where I harvested my raw material.

(*He begins to make relatively easy admissions.*)

Anyway, fathers were always shadowy figures, weren't they? What good do they serve...? Apart from stocking the pantry.

Oh, I admit I wasn't good at that either, even with financial help from my brother, Stannie ... at least not until my generous patron, Harriet Weaver, turned up. Then, we were able to live well ... dine in good Parisian restaurants, drink fine wines ... at least until *her* money ran out ... All right, I admit it, when there was money around, I spent it ... often on myself – voice lessons, opera tickets, Italian cigars, and of course, drink. I never claimed to be a saint...

(*Tops up glass.*)

I do regret that when we lived in Trieste, Nora sometimes had to take in washing ... I think it may have embarrassed her in front of the neighbours ... I suppose I wasn't a good provider ......

I was fond of my own father but he was hardly a family man either.

(*Looks at picture of his father.*)

And *he* wasn't obsessed by writing or distracted by any other form of activity ... except drink. So, what was *his* excuse? I managed to get on all right without a close father. Often, I preferred his absence to his presence.

(*Puts down picture.*)

There's a parallel here with colonies of course. When the ruling Empire departs, the newly freed colony has to stand on its own two feet, and make its own decisions for the first time. It has to start from scratch, conceive itself ... That's how Synge and I saw it, though Yeats took a different approach, going back into history, looking for faeries and the Celtic Twilight. The crucial point is that when you kill the father it's important to know what to do for an encore...

Anyway, I don't mean to be too defensive ... but what should I have done? There's no rule-book for parenthood.

I mean, could you imagine Stephen Dedalus – that rather pompous *aesthete* – being a good father? Horses for courses, after all, as The Citizen might say. Maybe if I'd stuck to medicine or to tweed-importing or running a cinema, I'd have been a better family man. Those more mundane jobs can be done without much emotional investment. Maybe I assumed that Lucia and Giorgio would be as independent as I was... Maybe this, maybe that... What if Adam had a navel...? What's done is done...

(*Tops up glass.*)

All right, I drank too much. Nora would say *far* too much ... and she used to give me hell for coming home drunk and waking the children. She said I often had four bottles of white wine of an evening. I would lose count after two and a bit, so maybe she's right. At least I packed in the absinthe and cocaine … I did like to sing … I can't deny that … So, maybe I did frighten the children, but I didn't mean to. Besides, most fathers come home drunk occasionally. And some of them beat the children … I never did that … At least I hope not.

And then, in the early years in Trieste, I brought over my brother, Stannie and, later, my sister, Eileen, to help out. Stannie was like a second father to the children. And he contributed to the household income. Did I exploit him? I don't think so. He was a free agent after all … So was Eileen.

(*He reverts to defensiveness and uses digressions to avoid real issues.*)

Drink never affected my work though. I was writing away the next morning, hang-over or not. Actually, the best cure for a hang-over is an obsession, something you can get stuck into. I liked drinking but was addicted to writing.

(*Pause, sits.*)

I hate my life now. Because of poor sight I had to give up writing. It's ironic, isn't it? I would have plenty of time for the children now, at this stage of my life … but they're not children anymore, and they don't need me, not even my grandson, Stephen.

Sam Beckett will probably always be childless. See how I'm digressing already? No, I don't want the court-scene structure. Too formal and rigid … too

Anglo-Saxon. My thoughts tend to babble and flow like a river … Sam, yes … I had hoped he might marry Lucia … Lucia … My poor daughter…

(*He becomes a little emotional, quickly changes subject.*)

Sam Beckett stayed in occupied France to do his bit in the war. He once told me he was stabbed by a pimp, and he was in a state of shock for quite a while. I said to him, "What chance will you have against Hitler?" I told him to go back to Ireland but he wouldn't hear of it. "I owe a debt to France," he said, more than once. An honourable man, with a sense of duty. Born a protestant of course. Yes, he would have been a fine son-in-law, and he gave me such help with the Wake … He was the love of Lucia's life … But it wasn't to be … Lucia ... She had no luck … (*Pause*)

As I said, I don't think I've much time left on this earth. Nora says I'll go on forever, as if *she* believes in eternal recurrence. But she's wrong. In Ireland you had to go around in circles because of the coastline … but not in Europe. Despite my poor eyesight, I see the end of the line coming up out of the mist. It's not that far away.

(*He finally begins to confront the issue.*)

I have to face up to things … now… Time is short … I suppose the question is: Did I put too much effort into these objects?

(*He looks at both books.*)

And did I do it ... at the expense of my children?

(*He stands and paces.*)

Thirty years of intense work, while they were young and may have needed a better father ... Lucia and Giorgio, I love them dearly.

(*Faces audience.*)

But these books drove me demented and left me blind. Everything I am, every part of me, went into these books. There was nothing left for anyone or anything else. Sex went out the window as I became more and more involved in Ulysses. Maybe Nora was relieved, I don't know ... "I can sleep better now," was all she'd say. My eyesight deteriorated, despite all those operations ... Twenty-three at the last count. The Wake robbed me of vision ... The sponge was squeezed dry and I couldn't dive anymore ... Language is so demanding, a fiendishly cruel mistress. ... *Experimenting* with language is a rough trade. It resists change, and often fights back in a fearsome way. The father tongue of Empire doesn't want to be killed, especially by the runt of the litter. Me. And then when you get into the irreducible atoms of language, the splicing and welding of quarks, there is no space left for anyone or anything ... except for drink. Wine wets the sponge.

(*He tops up glass.*)

Maybe writers should be celibates, like priests. Their job is not so different, turning ordinary material like bread into the transcendent. *Hoc est enim corpus meum.* And wine into blood. Red, not white.

Of course, anyone could have written Dubliners or even Portrait.

(*He lifts up Finnegans Wake and Ulysses.*)

But not these two. Oh no. These were mine, all mine. And I expect my readers to devote their lives to them. Nothing less. Why bother writing what anyone else could write?

(*Sits.*)

That brash young man, Hemingway, once advised me to keep it simple. "Gertrude Stein gave me that advice," he said, "and it stood to me, big time." I told him that simplicity was just the ticket … for the simple-minded. He was quite upset … But Eliot agreed with me. Density is the thing … texture … I'm digressing again … must focus…

(*Reluctantly, his thoughts turn to Lucia.*)

Lucia … Lucia, so like Nora in a way and also so different. Her lithe dancer's body and lovely dark eyes that she herself didn't care for. Sancta Lucia, bringer of light. That's what I called her whenever she brought me my spectacles. She probably doesn't know how much she helped me with Finnegans Wake. As a young girl, she used to dance in my study while I wrote. I followed her rhythm, her flowing movements, her dreams as far as I understood them … My deepseep daughter, flispering like a river at the beginning of its journey to the sea. So thoughtful and effervescent at the same time… She called me Babbo and she understood what I was about. I remember that time Harriet Weaver left me short of money … I came home early and, from the corridor I could hear Nora reading from the manuscript of Finnegans Wake. It was that passage about, 'woman with curlpins, trekant mouth, fithery wight' … Nora thought it was all gibberish but Lucia said that she followed it … sort of. She certainly identified with the flowing of the River Liffey out by Chapelizod. Nora was amazed by that, but I wasn't surprised. Lucia's heart was like a river close to its source, beating fast, as the river gathered up all its young and lively tributaries and began its long journey to the sea.

Lucia seemed happy then, bright and sunny. And cheeky too … oh, yes … she could knock you over with a look or a jibe… But, she had no way of knowing the disappointments that lay ahead. She was always impulsive and she liked to spar with her mother… Maybe it was more than sparring, who can tell? Nora favoured Giorgio over Lucia, I'm not sure why. With me it was probably the other way around. As parents we're not supposed to have favourites, but sometimes nature takes over and it can't be helped.

I'm not surprised that Sam Beckett fell for Lucia. I was jealous at first … I admit it. But deep-down I hoped it would work out between them. They were so well suited. Nora thought so too. And of course, so did Lucia. Poor Lucia, she never had a chance. Not even with her dancing; she just couldn't rise to the big occasion. She wanted to be the next Isadora Duncan, and she had the talent – more than enough…

(*He stands.*)

It's almost as if she wanted to fail … as if she didn't deserve success for some reason I can't fathom. She had so many huge disappointments in her young life… Every bond she made became a bond of sorrow.

(*He goes to the family portrait.*)

I can still see the marks where she tried to tear herself out of this picture. Said she … didn't belong … in this family, that she didn't … belong anywhere… I thought they were just words … Christ … I can't even get her out of France now, because of the war … and I can't visit her in the asylum because of the Nazis … (*Emotional*) … I'll die without seeing … I'll never see her again … my only daughter…

(*He tops up glass, drinks, and fights back tears. He feels so guilty about Lucia, he changes the subject to Giorgio.*)

And Giorgio … such a bright boy. So handsome and with such a good singing voice. A bass, not like my squeaky tenor… But so unsure of himself … didn't like singing in public. He accused me of parading him around so that he'd reflect well on me. Children can be so critical, and cruel without meaning to be. He also accused me of using Lucia and himself, *and* Nora, as material for my books … I can't deny that. But was it not a sign of love…? He didn't see it that way. Exploitation was the word he used. Exploitation. Said he and Lucia felt used … used and belittled … they weren't real people, only characters … worse, the raw material for characters … objects rather than subjects… That did hurt me.

(*He clutches his stomach and sits.*)

He also came to believe that Helen Fleischman only married him on the rebound. Was there something in that? I hope to God I did nothing to encourage her… Nora didn't like Helen one bit. She thought Helen flirted with me, and maybe she did, but it was all harmless… I thought Helen's wealth would finally bring some stability to Giorgio's life. She had a flat in Paris, a house in New York and another one in the Pyrenees, and she went around in a chauffeur-driven Rolls Royce. The age difference didn't bother him. There were so many things we couldn't afford to give Giorgio, or Lucia for that matter. Money may not buy happiness but it can provide a better class of misery. But I was wrong. Giorgio's marriage ended badly. In the final analysis, Nora was right about Helen. She told me I was as daft as a brush to think any differently.

(*Stands and opens another bottle.*)

I should have tried to reassure Giorgio. But where did his insecurity come from? I thought the experience of living in different European cities would have been good for him – and for Lucia. But he said they always felt rootless, as if they'd been dragged around from place to place. Forty-eight different homes, twelve different schools between Trieste, Pola, Rome, Zurich and Paris. He kept a tally, apparently. It surprised me greatly that he had those figures on the tip of his tongue, as if he often went over them in his mind… He said they felt like Gypsies … Gypsies…

Moving, and doing moonlight flits had become a habit to me, almost a way of life. My father was the same … in Dublin all those years ago, dodging creditors and landlords – after he drank every penny he had. I never knew what a settled home life was. The first time we skipped out of an apartment we had three hand-carts of clothes and furniture. The last time, we didn't even need a hand-cart – everything had been pawned…

Giorgio also said that he and Lucia were deprived of the chance of going to university, unlike me. "We're always in your shadow," he said, "trying to measure up in various ways: singing and dancing, and sketching … hoping you would be proud of us and not ashamed" … ashamed … my God, how could he have thought that…?

He announced out of the blue … in *Les Deux Magots,* I think it was … that he and Lucia were incoherent in three languages. Their knowledge of Triestene Italian was good but I can see how that made it difficult for them in Paris – school-work and so on. They probably found it hard to make friends. He said he and Lucia lived in one cage and I lived in another cage. A strange metaphor for any family … aaagh..!

(*He holds his stomach, sits.*)

Colitis acting up … maybe an ulcer … the pain will pass… Physical pain is not so bad … Dr. Fontaine doesn't think I need surgery … I wonder if she's right … I'll find another doctor when we get to Zurich.

Giorgio accused me more than once of being an alcoholic and told me in no uncertain terms that my drunken behaviour embarrassed him and Lucia, especially if friends and neighbours were present. I told him that he shouldn't feel embarrassed – because I didn't feel that, and because Paris was a Bohemian city that tolerated all kinds of odd behaviour. I don't think I ever got through to him.

As I said, I thought Helen would be the making of Giorgio, but I was so wrong. Some layer of harmful sediment must have been laid down in his childhood. He once said something very cruel to me … very cruel … He said that I wanted Nora to cheat on me … so that I could write about the feelings of jealousy … (*Pause*) ... Christ, he may not have been entirely wrong… That's what writing did to me. I was prepared to sacrifice everything to that bitch goddess.

Poor Giorgio took to the drink, not white wine which was my tipple. No, spirits, cognac, Irish whiskey – the hard tack. "Spirits are more efficient," he said once, "They make you numb faster." Maybe he wanted to out-do me … Irishmen like to out-drink each other to prove their masculinity… But it was bad for him, and for his marriage no doubt. And Helen, who turned out to be highly strung, has *also* ended up in an asylum.

What could I have done? I had to write… These so-called psychiatrists think up names for mental quirks that are merely eccentricities. A little bout of sadness *becomes* 'melancholia' … absent-mindedness *becomes* 'dementia', for God's sake … then hospital. It's a good racket. For psychiatrists … not their unfortunate patients. They even told Sam Beckett he had suffered a 'nervous breakdown'! Sam, of all people…

(*More avoidance.*)

Those thirty years went by so quickly … in a blur. These books … did I write them or raise them…? In any case, I was buried in these books. I slept with them and rose with them; they were in my waking and sleeping mind. One of them was about a day in the life of ordinary people. The other was a night in the dreams of extraordinary people. I covered it all, what Freud would call the conscious and the subconscious. From the particulars of life I was able to embrace the universals. I made epics out of all the detritus from the sea-floor, and, yes, from the people closest to me. I wanted to unify everything … 'all space time in a nut-shell'. I wanted not just to find the Philosopher's Stone, but to create it – the union of spirit and matter ... I was driven to hold in my arms the loveliness that had not yet come into the world... Not a bad day's work ... if I may say so myself ... though it took so many years. Maybe I earned the name: Artificer?

(*Reality begins to set in: He is drawn back to Lucia. This is his personal epiphany.*)

Artificer...? Some Dedalus I was....! Both my children crashed ... they crashed...! I can hear Lucia now ... I can't ignore her ... not again ... no ... not anymore.

(*He picks up the family portrait, weeps and tries to compose himself.*)

I don't think Lucia saw the break-up with Sam coming... She was badly undermined by it ... and I think she probably went off her medicine. I tried to involve her more in Finnegan's world – as a means of escape, I suppose. Sometimes it seemed to work. She seemed reasonably content in hiding out in the fantasy world. But she still suffered from nightmares – and some lack of fulfillment that was a mystery to me... She once told me that ... that ... she didn't exist ... I asked her what she meant by that, and she said ... "I'm not real." She said it so quietly, but there was conviction in her voice...

(*He sits down weakly.*)

I thought I knew how ... to comfort her, but when she went into a downward spiral ... I felt helpless. And then that awful set-back to her dancing career.

Nora used to tell her that her modern dancing looked cheap and that she should take up ballet... Lucia was far too old to start ballet... She couldn't cope with it... That was bad enough but the dance contest at the Bal Bullier was so unfair ... and poor Lucia took the decision so badly... "I've been beaten down again..." she said over and over ... "beaten down again..." It brought back all her upset about being born out of wedlock, all the memories of being mocked at school. She sometimes attacked Nora for making her a bastard... There were some terrible scenes. 'King Lear scenes' I called them, trying to lighten the mood ... as if I could... At those times I couldn't write a word.

I thought that when Nora and I got married to satisfy Helen's strait-laced parents, Lucia would get over that concern. But she didn't. She said, "Once a bastard, always a bastard."

Nora tried to tell me often enough that Lucia was ill. Hebephrenia was Jung's diagnosis, apparently. I couldn't accept it ... not mental illness. How could my lovely daughter be afflicted by an illness that was associated with ... with ... syphilis...? Not even Ibsen could mention that word in Ghosts. It is too horrible... What if I ... had been responsible ... if my blood had been contaminated...? No, no, it couldn't have been that... People are all different ... Lucia was merely impulsive... Of course her impulses sometimes upset others, but that's in the nature of things. Isn't it?

Lucia's disappointment was distressing to all of us.

Her frustrated longings were bad enough … but Nora sometimes hinted at something more serious, something unthinkable… Well, enough of that…

(*Sits and tries to rally himself.*)

I called Lucia my 'mignon' or my 'inspiratrice' or 'Nuvoluccia in her lightdress'. People looked askance at that, reading too much into those names. I never wanted her to go away from me. And if she did, I wanted her to return… "Sad and weary I go back to you my cold sad feary father." That was my dream … rêverons … riverrun. She was also Issy, the sprightly river running into the sea and being reborn. She taught me about dreams, the mind within, fantasy worlds… Naturally, I was furious when Jung gave that diagnosis … what did he know of her soul, the spark that lit her from within?

And then, when she went on holiday to Harriet Weaver in England there were some incidents and Weaver sent Lucia to an asylum. I'll never forgive her for that. It was the thin end of the wedge… Poor Lucia is now in a French asylum, and because of this damn war, I can't get to see her.

(*Stands and looks at the portrait.*)

Lucia wanted to get outside this frame … to soar … as high and free as her nature wished… But she needed stronger wings than the ones I made for her … much stronger…

I was so pleased when Lucia took up calligraphy and sketching. She could do all those wondrous

Celtic knots and stylised images of animals, the kind that appear in the Book of Kells. We were both drawn to swirls and circles – the commodious vicus of recirculation. I persuaded her to gather up all her drawings and then I had them published in this book called 'Chaucer's ABC'.

(*He goes to the suitcase and fetches the book. He looks lovingly at it.*)

We had a little celebration here *en famille*, and I presented the first copy of the book to her. It was meant to be a happy occasion but Giorgio and Nora weren't pleased … and Lucia was in one of her moods. I remember Giorgio saying she was catatonic. He attacked me. "Do you really think," he said, "Do you really think that a book will help Lucia in any way? Another damned book?" He said that Lucia should have been hospitalised years ago and that my refusal to do so had worsened her condition. He said I was terrified of the stigma of mental illness.

Later that same evening Nora accused me of always thinking about myself rather than of the family and that I had played God with them and with other people. She knew I didn't believe in religion but she said I should have tried at least to *behave* like a Christian. I tried to argue that the children inspired me and that it was natural that they would appear in my writing. But she said I had to see it from their side. She herself felt used when I based Molly Bloom on her. "You had no right to do that to me," she said, "no right to publish those intimate things…" It was one of the worst rows we ever had … but, thankfully, we got over it, and it didn't weaken the bond between us… The children are another matter…

(*He picks up Chaucer's ABC, puts it down, sits.*)

Lucia, my only daughter … I failed her… Only Giorgio could really comfort her. And he felt he should have done more even when he was a youth. He took the burden from my shoulders though he was little more than a child himself. Without his guidance Lucia would never have gone for treatment … *I* would never have sent her…

Once when she was prowling around the house, having woken from one of her nightmares, I heard him urging her to go back to bed. "You're so tired, Lucia … you must get some sleep…" He was so gentle with her. She said she was afraid … afraid to close her eyes because she might never wake… He tried to reassure her … "You will wake, Lucia," he said. "Don't worry." "No," she replied. "I won't wake. No…" But she went to bed anyway… (*Pause*) … and she hasn't awoken since … never will … not in that asylum.

(*He lowers his head and fights back tears. Standing, he notices something in the suitcase, bends to retrieve it. It is a soft toy.*)

This must have been Lucia's … I'm not sure … can't remember…

Once, I could forget deliberately … put things out of

my mind … but not anymore.

(*Puts doll back.*)

Once, I could refuse to listen … and do it with a clear conscience because of my work in all its demanding detail… After a long while, Nora gave me a fool's pardon.

(*Picks up portrait.*)

But I can't accept it … not now. I made a mistake … a lifelong mistake … I brought up my books instead of my children. They will never know how much I love them … because I never took the time to tell them…

I dragged those children around Europe but, worse still, they lost themselves because of me … I brought them into the fantasy world … *I* could come out of that world because I knew the way … both of my children closed their eyes … because they trusted me to be their guide … they trusted me … their father… And now they're lost and abandoned in that forest where I left them… I can still see their lovely faces… Forgive me … Lucia and Giorgio … forgive me…

(*He holds the family portrait to his chest and exits slowly.*)

Lights down.

END

CONTRAST

A Play in Two Acts

William John Leech (1881-1968)
A Convent Garden, Brittany, c.1913
Oil on canvas, 132 x 106 cm
National Gallery of Ireland Collection
Photo © National Gallery of Ireland

NOTES FOR ACTORS

ANGELA and DAN – a middle-class couple in their forties. They have not been communicating well for a few years. He has reluctantly learnt to live with it, but she is concerned about the future of their relationship and will fight to save it.

(ANGELA *is talking on her cell phone in the kitchen.*)

ANGELA: …I don't believe it, Deirdre … Dan got off at Pearse Street again…? And he went to the same place…? What's going on…? Almost an hour this time … Did he meet someone there…? He *is* acting strangely … I've noticed it … I'll really have to tackle him about it…
(*Sound of key in lock.*)
(*Startled*) Speak of the devil … Dan's at the door … must go. Thanks again, Deirdre … bye. Talk soon.
(ANGELA *clicks the phone shut.* DAN *enters wearing a suit and tie. He is carrying a designer briefcase. He is about to go to another room.*)
(*Anxiously*) Hello Dan ……

DAN: (*Formally*) Angela…

ANGELA: Oh, Dan…! Dan, I was … em … wondering … if we might talk…

DAN: I have work to … (*Reluctantly*) Now…?

ANGELA: Yes…

DAN: Well … em, all right…
(*He looks at his watch, leaves down the briefcase. They sit.*)

ANGELA: (*Tentatively*) How was your day?

DAN: Oh, the usual. SameO, SameO.

ANGELA: Boring?

DAN: There's nothing exciting about the auctioneering game in this market.

ANGELA: (*Pointedly*) Nothing at all?

DAN: What do you mean?

ANGELA: Dan, I have to ask you something…

DAN: What…?

(*Beat*)

ANGELA: Are you … are you … going to the office these days…?

DAN: What're you getting at…?

ANGELA: What's going on, Dan? You need to tell me.

DAN: Nothing's going on … why does everything have to be so dramatic…?

ANGELA: (*Upset*) I called the office yesterday … and the day before…

DAN: So? I was probably out … viewing property or something…

ANGELA: (*Loudly*) Please, Dan … For God's sake…!

(*Beat*)

DAN: All right! All right! Christ Almighty, OK … I've lost my job … I was going to tell you … when the time was right.

ANGELA: I knew it! I knew it was something like that… We're supposed to be a team. You should have told me.

DAN: A team? Yeah … well, I didn't want to worry you. I'm still trying to process it myself.

(DAN *stands and paces.*)

ANGELA: What reason did they give you?

DAN: Oh, the usual waffle about the recession. The real reason was that I should have sold more crap properties.

ANGELA: Why do you get off the train at Pearse

Street Station?

DAN: What…? Well, I have to see different people now … about jobs. Networking, you know…

ANGELA: (*Cautiously*) But you go into the National Gallery and stand in the same spot for ages.

DAN: (*Loudly*) What? What is this? Are you following me?

ANGELA: Not me.

DAN: Deirdre! Christ, why can't that woman mind her own business?

ANGELA: Why do you stand in the same spot in the Gallery? Are you … waiting for someone?

DAN: No, of course not…

ANGELA: Are you sure, Dan? Remember the last time you…? It's very important…
   (DAN *sits again.*)

DAN: I'm not waiting for anyone, Angela … I'm just … you know … looking at a painting…

ANGELA: A painting…

DAN: It's a painting that … sort of … caught my eye … William Leech is the artist…

ANGELA: 'A Convent Garden in Brittany' – painted around 1913.

DAN: Jesus! That bloody Deirdre! Did you ask her to tail me? Is she a private detective nowadays?

ANGELA: Well, what about the painting?

DAN: I'm sure you've googled it. Or Deirdre has!

ANGELA: A young novice in a walled garden. She's dressed in white lace because she's about to become a Bride of Christ. Who am I telling? It's a little holy for my taste. It obviously means something to you…

DAN: It's hard to say … I-I just like it … You know … It's good … a nice picture…

ANGELA: Nice…? It's more than that, Dan. You gaze at it almost every day. It must … speak to you in some way.

DAN: Look, I've lost my job and you're going on about some painting…

ANGELA: It's obviously not just 'some painting' to you … So, tell me what you see in it.

DAN: (*Uncomfortable*) Well, you know … it's bright … the figures sort of grow out of the white flowers … Delphiniums, I think they are … It's sort of … illuminating … sunlight on leaves and all that … A nice garden … What's not to like…?

ANGELA: (*Suspicious*) What about the main figure, the young novice nun in white lace?

DAN: She's very well painted … You have to hand it to the artist…

ANGELA: His second wife was the model. She's attractive…

DAN: …I suppose so … anyway it's all arty-farty stuff.

ANGELA: And she's dressed in white lace…

DAN: (*Bridles*) Ah now, come on … we're not talking romance here … or lingerie … nothing like that. Give us a break.

ANGELA: (*Keen*) So what does she represent?

DAN: You know, none of this really matters!

ANGELA: It does to me … I want you to tell me.

DAN: What's to tell? It's all just … art. I'm a real

estate agent, for God's sake … What do I
know? Come on, Angela … it doesn't matter!

ANGELA: (*Loudly*) Dan, will you please tell me
what the young nun means to you. (*Beat*) Tell
me … it's important … for us… Tell me
now…!

DAN: Jesus, enough!

(DAN *stands and paces. Angela stands too.*)

ANGELA: (*Loudly*) What does she mean?

DAN: She means … she means … well sort of … a
kind of … purity. There, are you happy?

ANGELA: What?

DAN: You heard me!

ANGELA: (*Disbelieving*) Purity…? Purity…?

DAN: You don't have to repeat it…! Look, she's in
this bright garden … ready to give up
everything … to devote herself … well, it's
sort of … beautiful … So now you know.
Satisfied?

ANGELA: But you're not religious…

DAN: It has nothing to do with religion. It's the
contrast. Don't you see? The contrast.

ANGELA: What on earth you talking about?

DAN: The contrast between my life and hers.

ANGELA: (*Frustrated*) Dan, what are you trying to
say?

(DAN *sits.* ANGELA *joins him.*)

DAN: (*Looks at her*) Look, I've spent most of my
adult life cheating and chiselling in one way or
another, selling sub-standard houses to young
couples desperate to get on the property ladder.
We didn't worry about phantom bids, or phony

guide prices… It was all bad … disgusting. I was in a tank of shit … and couldn't get out.

ANGELA: (*Thoughtful*) And this painting … helps you in some way?

DAN: It shows a young woman ready to give up the world… She's on her own in the garden, separate from the older nuns in the background… It's a pure moment. I can't explain it very well … time standing still … something to do with grace maybe…
(*He shrugs helplessly. Beat.*)

ANGELA: (*Thoughtful*) I didn't know you were so … that you could be affected like that … in that way…

DAN: When you lose your job there's time to think… My heart was never really in that job … I hated it…

ANGELA: (*Surprised*) I didn't know that … you never said … you never said anything…

DAN: Didn't I? I thought you knew … assumed maybe… Stupid I suppose…
(*Beat.* ANGELA *stands and begins to move slowly towards* DAN.)

ANGELA: I can't believe you didn't tell me any of this before… It sounds weird, but I feel as if … I don't know you very well … or didn't…

DAN: (*Calm*) I can't believe you had your busybody friends follow me around.

ANGELA: (*Remorseful*) I'm sorry. And I'm sorry you lost your job.

DAN: I'm not, not really. But things will be tough for a while. On you as well.

(*Beat*)

ANGELA: We'll manage.

> (ANGELA'S *face loses its worried expression.*
> *She puts her hand on Dan's shoulder.*)

DAN: I hope so.

ANGELA: Somehow.

DAN: Yes.

> (*His hand begins to move up towards hers.*)

ANGELA: We survived before.

> (*He covers her hand with his.*)

DAN: We did.

> (*Beat*)
> (*Both smile almost shyly. Lights down. The*
> *projected painting remains visible for a while*
> *and then slowly fades.*)

Lights down.

END

PRAYER

A One-Woman Play

An unnamed Italian woman of about forty reminisces about a major tragedy in her life. She is finally confronted by an ISIL executioner wearing a balaclava.

(*A woman is alone in a dark space. She delivers the following monologue.*)

I came to Iraq as a journalist in more peaceful days. I had met my husband in Rome, and when he was sent back to Baghdad I accompanied him with our beautiful baby girl, Christine. We later moved to a small town, Bartella, outside Mosul and were very happy for several years.

I fell in love with the country and the people and even learnt Arabic. I studied Islam too, and thought highly of the Quran, though it didn't quite replace the residual faith I had in Christianity. The religion you are taught as a child tends to stick – some of it anyway.

After the Americans invaded, my husband got involved in politics and grew apart from Christine and me. The last I heard, he had crossed into Pakistan. Apparently, American will not invade any country that has a nuclear weapon. I think he will be safe there. I have no ill-will towards him. He is Christine's father.

The American war changed everything. Americans know how to destroy but not how to rebuild. They prepared the way for ISIL. The more they wage war on terror, the more terrorists spring up like dragon's teeth.

Before the war we had some very good years, Christine and I. We went for gondola rides on the Tigris or took bigger boats as far south as Samarra and even Baghdad. We could see fish swimming in the river and storks and herons flying overhead or perching in the fig trees and olive groves that lined the banks. In the cities we loved visiting museums and looking at ancient Assyrian statues and the winged lions that used to guard the palaces of kings in Babylon and Nimrud.

At home we had a small garden where Christine played with her Persian Squirrel. She hung a chicken bone in a date palm so that he could get calcium by chewing it. She loved that squirrel, and cried bitterly when he died from old age. We wrapped the small body in white cotton and buried him under a liquorice bush. I remember making her favourite food – tashreeb chicken – that night, but she remained inconsolable. She really missed that little creature.

Then there were the bazaars – so colourful and exciting though Christine at first was embarrassed to see me haggle. But later on when she was seven, she was able to bargain even better than I was. She was good in school and loved physics. I felt that she might become a scientist or engineer. I knew she'd be up against male prejudice in most Arab countries. But I had a number of options including sending her to an

Italian University.

Christine. Christine … joy of my life. Her pale green eyes always wide and receptive. A lovely child in every sense. Light brown hair and honey skin. And such a good nature. Not a mean streak or devious bone in her body. She would never cut corners or follow the line of least resistance. She was blessed … a blessed daughter to me. Sometimes an expression or gesture would turn my heart over. I could literally feel my heart lurch as if she had reached into my chest and clasped it. I knew for the first time why generations of people believed the heart to be the seat of all emotions.

I remember teaching her to ride a bike in one of the dusty streets of Bartella. When we left the stabilizers off, I held the back of the saddle for her. And then came the moment when I let her go … She wobbled for a while and then she started to pedal and the distance from me widened … and widened… That evening she laughed and marvelled at her achievement. So did I, but the recollection of that growing distance stayed in the back of my mind. The day would come when she would leave me to begin her own life. I dreaded it … Christine meant everything to me … life itself. She was my life. She had no reason to believe the world was full of danger. And I wanted to protect her from that realisation for as long as I could.

I was still a journalist at this time though a

freelance one. A couple of Baghdad newspapers used my articles ... Topix and NINA. And Radio Dijla sometimes broadcast pieces of mine. Money was in short supply but we managed to get by. Needless to say there was no child support coming from Pakistan. My ex-husband had almost disappeared. I read somewhere that he had become active in a fundamentalist sect. For all I knew he could have joined ISIL.

When ISIL terrorists came to our town there was much fear and disruption. The State soldiers fled, leaving civilians undefended. The terrorists rampaged through the streets looting and firing at will. When they came to our house they accused me of being a Nasiri and a Kafir. I tried to explain that I was born a Christian but didn't have *any* strong religious beliefs. That made them more angry, and a couple of them accused me of being a kufrul-nifaak, a religious hypocrite of the lowest kind. They tied my hands and raided the kitchen. I was glad Christine was still at school. She had just turned nine. I thought the jihadis would whip me or punish me in some way, according to their version of Sharia law.

But ... to my eternal shame ... they raped me instead.

Three of them, taking turns ... while the others held me down by standing on my hands ... or keeping a knife to my throat.

I fought at first but finally had to submit. I was

torn and bleeding. The only thought that sustained me was that Christine was safe ... Her youth would be no protection from these brutes. She would not be home from school for another hour, or longer if the bus driver stopped at the markets for fruit.

When the last rapist finished with me he kicked me and spat in my face. When they left, I crawled towards my phone but quickly realised there was no one to call. The puppet government and police force would do nothing. If I managed to get to hospital there would be no one in the house when Christine got home. I lay on the tiles for a while and may have passed out.

Then I heard shouting. There was something wrong with the truck the soldiers were to travel in. They came back into the house, swearing and waving their guns around – vicious-looking automatic weapons.

Then, to my horror I saw Christine in the doorway, silent, unmoving, looking at me ... My heart froze ... I hoped she wouldn't be noticed ... I prayed for her safety ... I prayed to whatever god might listen that she would not come to harm.

One of the terrorists saw her and made a filthy remark. He reached out and pushed her down on the floor. I crawled over and tried to push him off her.

He hit me repeatedly and shouted to his friends,

"Fresh meat! Over here ... tasty veal!" Other soldiers came in. I heard Christine scream for me. I managed to put my arms around her and lock my hands behind her back. If I held her tightly enough I could protect her from them. Blows rained down on me but I wouldn't release my grip.

I felt her tears on my face ... I felt her heart beat against my heart. One terrorist pulled hair from my head but I wouldn't release my grip. A blow from a rifle butt made no difference. I don't know where my strength came from. They were not going to defile my daughter. Not while there was breath in my body. They tried to pull her away from me but I held her close with all my strength.

Then I felt her heart falter and breath escape from her mouth ... There was only one heart-beat ... Mine. Only one ... I gradually realised what it meant.

Jesus, forgive me ... I had suffocated my beloved girl. My blessed daughter.

I had killed Christine ... me ... her mother ... but at least she was safe from those rapists...

No, no ... not really ... one of them... The other soldiers turned aside...

An officer came and ordered them out. The truck had been fixed and the convoy was leaving for Mosul. I didn't care what happened next.

Christine was dead and her body had been defiled. My life was over too. I didn't even notice that a couple of soldiers had been left behind.

I lay beside her. Holding her body to mine. I prayed … I prayed to her … to her soul wherever it now wandered.

Hours passed. I felt her body grow cold and stiff, and still we lay together. I lost consciousness.

(*Lights down briefly.*)

(*Lights up. The woman is now in shackles.*)

When I came to, I screamed her name hoping it had all been a nightmare.

This wasn't my house. They had moved me to a cellar in some half-ruined building.

Christine's body was gone. I wept and begged the soldier on guard duty to tell me what had happened. I pieced it together. They had buried her in an unmarked grave. I would not be told where until the ransom was paid.

What ransom? I was worth nothing. The Italian government would not pay any ransom for my freedom. Did the jihadis not know that?

A few days later they realised I was worthless … I heard them cursing about it … I know they're going to kill me. Death has no fears for me since Christine departed the world. My last wish is to see the place where my daughter is buried … and if possible to be buried beside her. But that is too much to hope for. My faith does not extend to Heaven or a hereafter, so I know I will never see her again. In a few billion years when our galaxy explodes the dust of our bodies may mingle somewhere in the universe. We won't be aware of it. But that thought is all I have to cling to.

(*Lights down briefly.*)

(*Lights up but dim.*)

This is the day … the moment of my death. I can sense it. I will never know where Christine is buried.

(*A male figure in black, wearing a balaclava enters silently. He is carrying a large sheathed knife. He walks silently up to the woman from behind. She doesn't turn around.*)

I know you're there … do it … do it … as an act of love for your God. I'm sure He will appreciate the sacrifice you offer to Him.

(*He reaches forward and hands her a black hood.*)

No. No hood.

(*He puts a hand on her shoulders and tries to force her into a kneeling position.*)

No. I won't kneel.

(*He tries again.*)

I won't kneel!

(*He unsheathes a large serrated knife. He grabs her hair with his left hand and lifts it so as to expose her neck. He brings the knife to the side of her neck. She closes her eyes.*)

Christine … be with me … my blessed daughter … my life … my heart … Christine…!

Lights down.

END

NICK IN BOX

A One-Man Play

NOTES FOR ACTORS

NICK lives in a box-sized room in a busy shopping mall. On the outside the box looks like a computer, one that gives psychological advice. It is, of course, NICK who listens to the problems and gives the advice, pretending it is the computer that does so. Apart from that he has no contact with people and lives a hermetic life. But he has a past that he can't quite shrug off.

SCENE ONE

A sparsely furnished space. A table and chair, a low cot or sleeping bag, sundry kitchen items such as a saucepan, microwave and Primus stove. The left-hand wall has a slot and peephole. There is a small, half-hidden exit in the opposite wall and a small press near it. There is a microphone on the table and a laptop. A child's drawing of a house and garden is pasted to the back of the laptop. The people who speak to NICK *are all offstage; their voices are pre-recorded.*

(NICK *is seated at the table with a mug of tea in front of him. He speaks to the audience.*)

NICK: I can talk to you because you're not part of my world. There's no need for a wall here between us because we'll never meet again. But do you see the walls on the other three sides? There are hundreds of people behind those walls. I know they're there, but I don't know anything about them and neither do you. They have no idea I'm in here. They're out there shopping in the mall. Retail therapy they call it. But many of them are sick in the head. And they come to me for help. They don't know it's me of course. They think I'm a computer. That wall there with the slot and the peephole is done up on the outside to look like the front of a large computer. If they want to talk to the computer … ME … they have to push money through that slot. Stick around and you'll see how it works.

You're all privileged in a way because you're being let in on the secret. The other three-quarters of the population out there are being kept in the dark. Are they being exploited? I don't think so. But you are the lucky ones. You're sane. You prefer theatre to retail therapy. You have the inside knowledge. Hermetic lore. You'll never meet the others, so the secret is safe. Safety is what it's all about. This is my safe place, as they say nowadays. As you know, there was a time when people were smarter than computers but that may not be true anymore. I'm in here pretending to be a computer. It's a turn up for the books, isn't it? I make good money too because lots of people find it easier to relate to what they think is a machine than to another human being. Very odd. Well maybe not so odd. I mean the internet is now our global brain. It may even be a new god – one that we created … I don't think I could live without my laptop. There's nothing else to believe in, is there? But I don't use social media. No. Privacy is important to me. I live in this box after all.

I had a very busy morning but this afternoon has been slow enough … uh … oh,

commentator's jinx … something's stirring.
(*He watches money being pushed through the slot in the wall. He talks into the mic in a formal, staccato, computerised voice.*)
Insufficient funds. If you want the short session please insert another five euro.
(*A five euro note comes through the slot.*)

NICK: Your session commences now at 8.15 p.m. Please state your name and the nature of your problem.

LORNA / VOICE: I'm … Lorna … Connors … I … I'm deeply upset because my … my husband…
(*She begins to weep.*)

NICK: You must state the nature of your problem. I am listening.
(*He pours himself another cup of tea.*)

LORNA: My husband … walked out on me…

NICK: Did he give any reason?

LORNA: No … He just got up from the breakfast table one Saturday morning … In the middle of his müesli … said he was going for a walk … but he never came back…

NICK: Why do you think he did that?

LORNA: I have no idea … he had no reason to leave… None.

NICK: Think carefully, Lorna.
(*A beep sounds.*)

NICK: You have five minutes left. Proceed.

LORNA: I think … he was playing away… But that's not my fault.

NICK: I am sure that is correct. But how do you know it's not your fault?

LORNA: (*Loud*) Because I didn't introduce him to that whore! And I did everything for him... Oh, there may have been other issues...

NICK: You seem like a good person, Lorna. But your time is up. I would recommend another session next week.

LORNA: But! But...!

(NICK *switches off the sound system and turns to the audience.*)

NICK: You probably think I was too abrupt with that woman, but she'll be back. It's not unusual for early sessions to go badly. The clients go away and think about their feelings. They usually return and then we begin to make progress... I have no qualifications in psychology. But still many people prefer to come to me instead of shrinks. Strange isn't it? You see, people believe in technology nowadays. They have more faith in computers than in professional people or even in God. Maybe this belief started with the Internet – I don't know ... I'm not a healer but by pretending to be a high-tech voice-recognition machine, I have some kind of power over the clients. By believing that I'm a machine they are basically healing themselves. It's all very strange ... a black box or some kind of conjuring trick. I've been in here for a couple of years now. I suppose I've no real life of my own ... I used to have but that's another day's work... Anyway, I like listening to the stories of clients. I can kind of live through all those small narratives.

I sneak out to the shopping mall on Saturdays to do my own shopping. I hang a 'Being Serviced' sign on the front of the computer – on the other side of that wall. I have a good lunch in one of the cafés out there. No one knows me – which is fine. Then I come back here and open for business once again. Maybe I'm turning into a machine! But that wouldn't be the end of the world, would it?

(*He laughs then cranes to listen.*)

Unless my ears deceive me, the mall is closing. Time for bed.

(*He gets into the sleeping bag with his laptop. Lights dimmed. He lights a small lamp and starts to read.*)

Good story this. Language they say can mean anything. That's OK. I take my own meaning out of it. I'm a very slow reader because I don't want to get to the end … so that's enough for me tonight. I'll think about that one sentence. I'll mull it over … good night, everybody.

(*He closes the laptop, looks at the child's drawing for a while, and switches off the lamp. In the darkness there are sounds of sobbing.*)

Lights Down.

SCENE TWO

(NICK *is up and about. He is sweeping his living area. He talks to the audience.*)

NICK: I just had an interesting client ... a man who can't sleep because of memories of an abusive childhood. A sad case. I hate it when children ... are deprived of ... childhood... It's ... so ... wrong... This man was on before and we had a slow start. But this time I think we may have made a little bit of progress. He poured his heart and soul out. It's probably easier to do that to a machine than to another human being. I'd certainly find that easier. You see the machine is not going to judge you. And it's not going to manipulate you because it doesn't have an agenda. So the client trusts the machine, and all fears and worries and self-loathing come tumbling out. Like colonic irrigation. I just give the odd prompt, but mainly listen. I told him he was a good person and should not blame himself. He cried his eyes out because he never believed that. And no one ever told him that... Of course it's nothing to do with me. I'm a nonentity. It's the whole set-up – machine, voice of authority, placebo effect – the whole ball of wax. Still, it's kind of satisfying when things begin to go right. Especially nowadays when people are sceptical about everything.

Oh and by the way, in case you were wondering, I pay the owner of the shopping mall for this little corner every month. Slide an envelope under his door. I'm sure he thinks I live in the city somewhere, not here in this 'computer'. I don't know what I'd do if it ever got out that I lived in here in this 'Chinese Box'. They'd probably call me The Phantom of the Mall or The Ghost in the Machine, or something like that.

Of course when I say 'he', the owner of the mall, I'm referring to an institution known as a vulture fund. Nobody knows who owns what anymore. Funny that because we're inundated with information, but not the important stuff. Uh … oh , business calls.

(*He sees money coming through the slot. He sits with the sweeping brush resting on a knee and switches on the mic.*)

NICK: (*Computer voice*) Your session begins now at 9.43 a.m. Please state your name and the nature of your problem.

VOICE / MELISSA: Melissa Stapleton … I'm accused of being a home-wrecker by a woman who's lost her marbles.

NICK: A home-wrecker? Did you have an affair with her husband?

MELISSA: Yes, but I didn't know he was married. He lied through his teeth. I … thought I was helping him… He was in a bad way … depressed … suicidal, I'd say. He'd lost so much … including a child…

NICK: Then it wasn't your fault.

MELISSA: Maybe I should have seen the signs, asked more questions.

NICK: Did you love this man?

MELISSA: Yes. At that stage. Before…

NICK: Love sometimes makes us blind. We project our wishes onto the loved one. Do not blame yourself.

MELISSA: Thank you. But his wife, ex-wife, keeps attacking me … calls me a whore. She makes me feel guilty…

NICK: I know it's difficult. But you must not take her seriously. I know that you are a woman of conscience, that you have sound values. Promise me not to blame yourself.

MELISSA: I … I…

NICK: Promise.

MELISSA: I … promise.

NICK: Good. That is the first step, Melissa.
　　(NICK *looks at his watch.*)

NICK: Don't hesitate to contact me again if you need to, Melissa. I am always here for you.

MELISSA: Thank you … thank you…
　　(NICK *switches off the mic.*)

NICK (*To audience*) See? I think my few words there did a little bit of good. All clichés of course. But they work. They're like little posies of snowdrops … aaaaawwwwww! You see, most people are insecure. They have low opinions of themselves. And there are no values anymore… So that's where I come in. I

give them compliments. They think the
compliments are coming from a machine and
must be reliable. They wouldn't believe them if
they came from a flawed human being.

And I'm kind of upbeat anyway. Why? You
might ask. Can a recluse be happy? Well, I
think so. One reason is that I'm self-employed.
I have no boss. I used to have bosses. Morons
… baboons. Completely up themselves. Some
couldn't make a decision to save their lives.
Others could but made the wrong decisions and
then tried to blame their 'subordinates' as they
called them. All psychopaths if you ask me.
Unable to understand other peoples'
problems… Well, that's my rant for the day.
(*He starts to clean a saucepan.*)
"I'm a rambler, I'm a gambler,
I'm a long way from home
And if you don't need me
Just leave me alone.
I'll eat when I'm hungry,
I'll drink when I'm dry
And if you don't kill me
I'll live till I die."
That's how I like it, folks. Farmers don't have
bosses. Their only boss is Nature and no one
quibbles with Nature. Bosses came on the
scene after the Industrial Revolution when
people got together in factories and had to be
supervised. And that's when anxiety began and
people started having nervous breakdowns and
going to shrinks. A lot of the people who come

to me have been badly damaged by the boss class. One man needed time off … for domestic reasons … serious reasons … but his boss made him work instead. Even though … even though … well, enough of that.

So you see it's win-win in here. I'm better off and I help others to improve their lives too. I don't even have to look at them. I hardly ever use that peephole over there.

(*He notices money coming through the slot.*)
Excuse me. Duty calls.

(*He speaks into the mic.*)
Your session commences at 10.14 a.m. Please state your name and the nature of your problem.

VOICE / TONY: My name is Tony Conlon and I suffer from anxiety.

NICK: Could you describe the symptoms of this anxiety?

TONY: I feel that a lot of people are trying to cheat me. It really gets under my skin.

NICK: What exactly do you mean by cheat?

TONY: Take advantage of me.

NICK: That usually happens only to good people, Tony – those with kind natures.

TONY: Look, I don't need reassurance … I don't have low self-esteem. I just want to let these bastards know that I'm not to be taken for granted. I'm not to be exploited.

NICK: I understand. But it's not your fault Tony…

TONY: I know it's not my bloody fault. It's the fault of all those yahoos and yobs I have to deal with. They don't play fair…

NICK: Your minimum session has expired. Please insert another five euro to…

TONY: Oh fuck off, you heap of junk.

NICK: That does not compute … session terminated for lack of funds.

(*To audience*) Well, there's always one, I suppose. He's full of anger. Sounds like a boss to me. When he settles down he may be back. I can tell him how to use his anger in more constructive ways. You know, if that had been me out there I think I'd have given the 'computer' a kick or a thump. But the average citizen doesn't do that. People have such respect for machines nowadays. It's as if we … I mean machines … are sacred objects.

(*He pours himself a cup of tea and fetches a biscuit from a drawer in the table.*)

Elevenses – such a civilised invention. I see I'm getting short on biscuits and other stuff … of course this is Saturday! I'd better do my shopping in a little while. I might have a burger out there as well. What else do I need? Cereal and washing-up liquid and paraffin for the stove. I don't need a list. I'll remember when I'm out there. Yeah, maybe I'd better go now before the crowds descend on the mall.

(*He collects a reusable shopping bag, the 'Being Serviced' sign, and money from the drawer. He combs his hair forward and puts on a pair of dark glasses and a cap.*)

This leads into a handy air duct over by the

anchor grocery store. Excuse me for a moment. Be back soon. Don't go anywhere.

(*He approaches the exit, which is only about two and a half feet high, on his knees, and crawls through it. When he is through, he pulls the little door after himself.*)

Lights down.

SCENE THREE

(NICK *crawls in through the little entrance, closes and bolts the door. He puts his groceries in a small cheap-looking press standing on the floor. He places the 'Being Serviced' sign on the table along with his dark glasses and cap.*)

NICK: Thank goodness the shopping is over for another week. I have enough müesli for a month... All those people ... God, the negative vibrations in the shops. I could feel the energy being leached from my bones. Vampires feeding on my blood. I still want to help them though, even if I can't face them. You see if everyone improved they might not have to feed off each other. I'm so glad to be back here ... in my space. I'm at a place where I need this space ... oh, I see I just got back in time. (*Money comes through the slot. Nick speaks into the mic.*) Your session commences at 2.11 p.m. Please state your name and the nature of your problem.

VOICE / LORNA: Lorna Connors. I spoke to you before. My husband walked out on me...

NICK: Yes. You are in my memory bank, Lorna. You were very upset. Rightly so. You are a good person.

LORNA: Oh, I may have been partly to blame.

NICK: No, You are not to blame, Lorna.

LORNA: I may have driven him away.

NICK: I do not believe so. Many men feel in a rut and behave badly. Sometimes they are depressed and feel trapped. They may have other issues. It's not your fault. You are a good person.

LORNA: How do you know? I could be a total bitch.

NICK: I know you are not a total bitch. You are a kind forgiving person, Lorna.

LORNA: Did a woman called Melissa Stapleton contact you?

NICK: (*Surprised*) I could not … I am not at liberty to discuss other clients.

LORNA: What a cheek that woman has. Anyway, back to me. You think I'm a good person?

NICK: Yes.

LORNA: Don't I owe you more money?

NICK: Oh yes. Please put another five euro in the slot.

(*The note comes through.*)

LORNA: If I'm such a paragon why would my husband leave me. If you were married to me would you want to leave?

NICK: Lorna, I'm a computer. The answer to that hypothetical question is not in my algorithms.

LORNA: You and your algorithms. Just answer one question for me.

NICK: Certainly, if I'm programmed for it.

LORNA: (*Quickly*) Do you like müesli?

NICK: Yes … no…! It does not compute. The session is over.

(*He switches off the mic and looks out the peephole.*)

Christ, false name … how did she find out? Maybe it's not her. But it is … it is… Oh fuck what's her next move?

(*He paces back and forth, distressed.*)

I was free in here when no one knew. But now I'm trapped. Have to move on. No, God knows what's out there. Happy here. Not happy but content. Oh it's all gone haywire. Calm down. Deep breathing. There's no computer I can turn to. God grant me the serenity to … something … something and wisdom to know the difference…

She may decide to let sleeping dogs lie. I put money into her account when I left. Nearly all the money I earned from those movies. Maybe she'll decide to leave me alone. She couldn't want me back… Not after the mistake I made with Lisa… Christ, was that Melissa by any chance…? Does *she* know I'm in here as well? Jesus, it's all coming apart…! They're closing in on me…

(*He shows alarm when he hears knocking.*)

VOICE / TONY: It's over.

NICK: Please insert money…

TONY: We're gone past that. The game is up.

NICK: Please state your name and the nature of your problem.

TONY: Nice try, Nick. I've been talking to your

wife. She says she's reconciled to your
daughter's death. It was one of those accidents.
She says you don't have to blame yourself
anymore. Open up.

NICK: I have no option but to terminate…

TONY: Listen Nick, it's Tony here, your landlord.
It's obvious you need treatment. I heard all
about you and your breakdown. And I'm sorry
about what happened to … your family … I
am. But you're not entitled under the lease to
live on the premises. Health and safety
regulations… Now open up or I'm going to
have to break in.

(NICK *rushes to barricade the small entrance
with the press.*)

TONY: Pass me the hammer. We'll soon get this
little hermit crab out of his shell.

NICK: I can't go out there! I can't face it!

(NICK *rushes back and forth in a panic. When
he hears sounds of hammering he sinks to the
floor. He rocks slowly in that position. He looks
at the child's painting, and holds the laptop to
his chest.*)

No. No. No. Leave me alone … please leave us
alone … we're not doing any harm.

(*He continues to rock and clutch the laptop as
the sounds of hammering intensify.*)

Lights down.

END

THE WRONG ADDRESS

A Play for Radio

NOTES FOR ACTORS

BRENDAN'S lovely daughter, SHEILA, is about to get married and he has to confront a secret that has haunted him for many years. He is advised by his brother, JIM, and hassled by his wife, MAURA. He is upset by some of the wedding guests and by memories of his past.

SCENE ONE

Interior: Cafe at lunchtime, muffled conversation in background, sounds of meals being served, faint mood music.

JIM: What's wrong with you Brendan? You're sitting there with a face like a wet week.

BRENDAN: Well … it's Sheila's wedding…

JIM: So? Your only daughter's nuptials. You should be happy. She's got a decent bloke there in Mark.

BRENDAN: It's not that, Jim…

JIM: What is it then?

WAITRESS: Who's the coffee?

JIM: Me.

WAITRESS: You must be the tea then.
(Waitress lays down cups and leaves.)

JIM: Well?

BRENDAN: (*in a rush, garbled*) I'll have to make a bloody speech.

JIM: What?

BRENDAN: (*louder, aggressively*) I'll have to make a bloody speech.

JIM: Aagh, I get it. The old problemo. I thought you grew out of that.

BRENDAN: Well, I didn't.

JIM: How about at work? Did you never have to make a presentation or…?

BRENDAN: (*surly tone*) No. I got others to do it.

JIM: Good God! They probably got the credit for your designs. I've heard of avoidance but this is ridiculous. And that's why you never got … em…

BRENDAN: Promoted? All right. All right. I'm a wimp and a failure.

JIM: Of course you're not. But look, it's only a sort of phobia… Don't let it ruin a great day. You don't *have* to make a speech.

BRENDAN: I'm the father of the bride … I have to.

JIM: Sheila will understand. And Maura.

BRENDAN: (*quietly*) They don't know about … it.

JIM: What? You've been married twenty-five years and they don't know? I don't believe it.

BRENDAN: OK, so it's my guilty secret. Big deal. But now I'm going to be caught out. Have your laugh.

JIM: I'm not laughing. Look, couldn't I do it? As uncle of the bride.

BRENDAN: Of course not. It's up to me. Me!

JIM: Write out a few words and just read them off. Everyone'll be too drunk to care. Have a few drinks yourself.

BRENDAN: I can't. I'm a teetotaller.

JIM: Oh yeah, I'd forgotten. How did we grow up so different? Well, look, just read out a few words. Imagine everyone is in the nude.

BRENDAN: Thanks, Jim. Thanks a lot.

End of Scene One

SCENE TWO

Exterior. Garden of family home, birdsong.

MAURA: (*opening back door*) Sheila, what are you doing out here in the garden?

SHEILA: Oh … just remembering things, Mam. You know how it is.

MAURA: (*emotional*) Come here, and give me a hug… (*They embrace.*) England isn't that far away… You'll be able to visit whenever you like. This is your home, Sheila. There'll always be a welcome here for you and for Mark.

SHEILA: I know, Mam… Do you remember my swing on that tree by the shed?

MAURA: I do indeed. Your Dad planted that tree the day you were born and he put up the swing on your tenth birthday.

SHEILA: I always loved playing here. Wasn't there a sandpit too?

MAURA: Yes. There, look, where the grass is still yellowish. You used to make sandcastles. We thought you might be a draughtsman … draughtsperson, like your Dad.

SHEILA: Was he disappointed when I did nursing?

MAURA: No, of course not. (*Claps hands, becomes businesslike.*) Look at the time! We'll have to get you into your glad rags. The wedding dress is on your bed. I'll give you a hand.

SHEILA: Remember now, no fuss.

MAURA: Who me? Fuss? I don't know what you mean.

SHEILA: Is Dad up yet?

MAURA: No, I think we'll let him have a lie-in. He didn't sleep well last night. He was up pacing around the bedroom.

SHEILA: Nerves?

MAURA: I don't really know… Now, chop, chop. We have to beautify ourselves and I have to double-check the arrangements. (*Door opens and closes*.)

End of Scene Two

SCENE THREE

Interior. Bedroom.

BRENDAN: (*Beginning to wake up. Thoughts*) No work today … ah great … have another little snooze … then bring the dog for a walk and get the paper … (*smacks lips, rolls over*) no … something else … what is it? Something different … oh God the wedding … speech. (*panicky thought rehearsal*) "Reverend Fathers, ladies and gentlemen … this is a great … wonderful day which we've all looked forward to … ever since Sheila and Mark announced their engagement … special thanks to Father Joe … on behalf of Maura and myself … delighted to welcome Mark into the family." Won't be able to get through it. All those people looking at me, sizing me up. Can't do it. Can't, can't… But I have to. (*Gets out of bed, pads around the floor.*) Where did I leave the bloody thing? Sock drawer. (*Opens drawer, folds out paper.*) "Reverend Fathers, ladies and gentlemen… This is a wonderful day…" Oh Christ, head splitting now. Have to go to the bathroom. (*rapid steps, opening door*)

End of Scene Three

SCENE FOUR

Interior: Sheila's bedroom.

MAURA: I'll just put a pin there below the bodice.

SHEILA: Make sure it's not visible. (*knock on door*)

MAURA: Brendan, is that you?

BRENDAN: Who were you expecting?

SHEILA: Morning, Dad.

BRENDAN: Morning, Sheila.

MAURA: You can't come in. Sheila's getting dressed. Have you had your shower? Did you wash your hair?

BRENDAN: Yes. Yes.

MAURA: Have you put on your morning suit?

BRENDAN: Not yet. That won't take long.

SHEILA: There's a pot of tea in the kitchen, Dad.

BRENDAN: OK. Thanks.

MAURA: Will you check the car people? The limousine has to be here at ten. On the dot.

BRENDAN: Right, anything else?

SHEILA: Are you all right, Dad. Not nervous or anything?

BRENDAN: How do you mean, nervous?

SHEILA: Mam said you didn't sleep much last night.

BRENDAN: I'm grand … grand. Bit of a toothache, that's all.

MAURA: The car people…

BRENDAN: I'm going. (*slippered footsteps going down stairs*)

End of Scene Four

SCENE FIVE

Interior: Kitchen

BRENDAN: (*on phone*) … so the car'll be here at
ten sharp and you have the address… Yeah,
that's it. OK thanks. (*Replaces phone. Pours
tea. Stirs it. Sips.*)
(*thoughts*) I wish this day was over … What
kind of a father am I? Self-centred … vain. Just
like Brother Matthias said…
(*Flashback to schoolroom. Hollow acoustic in
an empty hall.*)

BROTHER MATTHIAS: Now the other Canavan
boy, Brendan, will tell us what he did on his
holidays. Come up here Brendan to the top of
the class so we can all see you. (*slow footsteps*)
Now stand on that table. Go on, up you get.
(*sounds of footsteps on table*) Can you all see
him, class? Good. Now, off you go, Brendan,
with your narrative.

YOUNG BRENDAN: I … I…

BROTHER MATTHIAS: Yes? Yes? We're waiting
for your account.

YOUNG BRENDAN: I c-c-can't, Sir…

BROTHER MATTHIAS: You c-c-can't what?
(*titters from class*)

YOUNG BRENDAN: Can't … say…

BROTHER MATTHIAS: Straighten up. Face the

class. How do you mean you can't say? You've got a tongue in your head, haven't you?

YOUNG BRENDAN: Yessir…

BROTHER MATTHIAS: A tongue is for speaking isn't it?

YOUNG BRENDAN: Yessir.

BROTHER MATTHIAS: Don't turn sideways. Stand up and face your audience. Don't be a coward. You're not a coward are you, Brendan? Or a Mammy's boy?

YOUNG BRENDAN: No … Sir.

BROTHER MATTHIAS: Would you prefer the leather?

YOUNG BRENDAN: Yessir.

BROTHER MATTHIAS: Well, you're not going to get it. You can stay standing there until you tell the class all about your summer holidays. We'd all like to hear about that, wouldn't we, class? All about the adventures Brendan had in Fethard-on-Sea.

CLASS: Yessir. (*laughter*)

BROTHER MATTHIAS: I'll even help you. Start with: "We had a great summer in Fethard-on-Sea." Go on.

YOUNG BRENDAN: We … had … a…

BROTHER MATTHIAS: You see class. He can't even repeat that. Do you know why?

CLASS: Nossir.

BROTHER MATTHIAS: Do you know why, Mick Sinnott.

MICK SINNOTT: He's shy, Sir.

BROTHER MATTHIAS: No, Sir. He's not shy, Sir.

He's *vain*. He thinks everyone is sizing him up.
He's so vain he doesn't want to say anything in
case you'll think he's stupid. That's vanity.
He's vain and full of himself. What is he?

CLASS: Vain and full of himself, Sir.

BROTHER MATTHIAS: Well, Mr. Brendan-full-of-
himself-Canavan, you can stay standing on that
table all day … until your tongue loosens…

End of Scene Five

SCENE SIX

Interior: Kitchen

MAURA: (*opening door*) Brendan, Brendan! For
    God's sake you're not dressed yet.
BRENDAN: What? Oh yeah.
MAURA: Sheila, come in for a second…
SHEILA: What do you think, Dad?
BRENDAN: (*stunned*) Sheila … you look …
    wonderful. I … can't … just wonderful.
    (*Thoughts*) It's her day and I'm thinking about
    myself. Vain. Vain.
MAURA: Don't hug her. You'll crumple the dress.
    Go on. Run upstairs and throw on the suit.
    Quickly.
BRENDAN: Right. I'm going. (*footsteps*)
MAURA: I don't know what's got into him. The
    bouquet is on the hall table, Sheila. We mustn't
    forget that.
SHEILA: I've ticked off everything on my checklist.
    We're all set.
MAURA: Nervous?
SHEILA: (*laughing*) No. Should I be? We were
    shacked up for over a year.
MAURA: (*mock sternly*) I don't want to hear that.
    You bold thing. (*Laughs despite herself.*)

End of Scene Six

SCENE SEVEN

Exterior. Getting into the limousine. Car doors opening and closing. Sounds of driving.

MAURA: Driver, we've to be at St. Dominic's Church by 11 sharp.

DRIVER: Yes, Ma'am. No problem. (*sound of car moving off; faint sounds of traffic*)

MAURA: Sheila, mind your train. Spread it out a bit. Brendan, straighten your tie for God's sake.

BRENDAN: (*thoughts*) The die is cast now. No going back. Trapped. How can they be so calm. "Reverend Fathers, ladies and gentlemen… This is a wonderful … "

MAURA: What are you looking for?

BRENDAN: What do you mean?

MAURA: You keep rummaging in your inside pocket.

BRENDAN: Oh just some notes.

MAURA: Money?

BRENDAN: No. Notes … for a speech.

SHEILA: You won't go on for too long, will you, Dad? It's a fairly young crowd.

BRENDAN: Thanks.

MAURA: You didn't make a speech at our weeding.

BRENDAN: Didn't I?

MAURA: No.

BRENDAN: Maybe the etiquette was different then.

(*thoughts*) Liar. You funked it.

MAURA: I hope the catering is up to standard. God, what if Uncle Barney drinks too much? Mark's family shouldn't get the wrong impression.

SHEILA: Just because they're English, Mam, doesn't mean they're snobs. They're not.

MAURA: That's not what I meant. I hope the video fella is reliable.

BRENDAN: What's that about a video?

SHEILA: The whole show is being videoed.

BRENDAN: The speeches as well...?

SHEILA: Of course. Everything. A permanent record in living colour.

MAURA: Brendan, don't use your pocket handkerchief. If you want to mop your brow, here use a tissue.

SHEILA: Here we are. St. Dominic's. There's no going back now.

MAURA: Driver, pull over please. (*sound of engine slowing down*)

SHEILA: There's no sign of Mark or his family. (*laughs*) I hope I'm not being jilted.

MAURA: We're too early, dammit. We'll have to circle around. Brendan, you get out and give us a signal when we come round again. Wave us down if the groom has arrived.

BRENDAN: But...

MAURA: Out you get. Now. (*Car door opens and closes, limousine moves off.*)

End of Scene Seven

SCENE EIGHT

Gravel crunches as Brendan walks towards church.
Birdsong.

JIM: How're you, Brendan? (*Meaningfully*)
    Everything OK?
BRENDAN: Yes.
MALE GUEST: Big day, old son…
JIM: Where've Maura and Sheila gone?
BRENDAN: Into orbit. They don't want to arrive
    before Mark and his family.
JIM: But *they're* already in the church. Inside.
    Typical isn't it? The Brits are inside saying
    their prayers and the Paddies are out here
    having a last fag.
BRENDAN: What…? (*footsteps as the best man,*
    CHARLIE, *comes out of the church*)
CHARLIE: (*English accent*) Any sign of Sheila, Mr.
    Canavan? It's ten past the hour.
BRENDAN: They'll be here in a minute, Charlie…
    Have you got the ring?
CHARLIE: Yes. Don't worry about that.
    Everything's under control. Oh, and by the
    way, at the reception I'll give you as much
    notice as I can before your speech.
BRENDAN: Thanks.
CHARLIE: I'd better go back inside. The natives
    are getting restless. (*footsteps*)

JIM: No flies on that young man. Mark is even more relaxed… Look, here comes the limo. Better wave them down. (*Limousine stops. The two women get out.*)

BRENDAN: They were inside all the time.

MAURA: Good. We're late.

JIM: I'll pop in and cue the organist. (*footsteps*)

MAURA: Let me just straighten your veil.

SHEILA: Right, Dad? Ready to give me away?

BRENDAN: As ready as I'll ever be. Take my arm. (*Footsteps; organist plays 'Here Comes the Bride'. Appreciative murmurs from congregation.*)

MARK: (*English accept, whisper*) Sheila, you look … radiant.

SHEILA: (*whisper*) You're not too bad yourself, lover.

End of Scene Eight

SCENE NINE

Interior of church.

FATHER JOE: … and do you, Sheila, take Mark
George Taylor to be your lawful wedded
husband?

SHEILA: I do. (*sound of* MAURA *sniffling*)

BRENDAN: (*thoughts*) Wish I could cry too. Won't
remember any of this. Sheila is married. Can't
believe it and they're all standing there, so
relaxed. In full view. Time passing too quickly.
No way out now. Can't concentrate. What's
wrong with me? Wish I were a million miles
away. Or safe in my little office… And that
man with the video camera. He'll be at the
reception too.

FATHER JOE: … and I would also say to Sheila and
Mark that whatever difficulties they may
encounter in their life together, they will
always have God's grace to help them. For
marriage is a sacrament. They have made a
sacred commitment to each other. Their parents
and friends should be proud of these two young
people. It is a joyous occasion…

BRENDAN: (*thoughts*) It is. It is. Why can't I feel
it? God Almighty…

End of Scene Nine

SCENE TEN

Interior. Hotel Function Room. Buzz of chatter, sounds of meals being served.

MAURA: Oh it's great to be sitting down at last. My feet are killing me.

CAROLINE: (*English accent*) I know how you feel, Maura. Weren't we lucky the rain and wind held off for the outside photographs? … And how are you, Brendan? I'm so looking forward to your speech. The Irish are so witty. Father Joe's sermon will be a hard act to follow.

BRENDAN: We can but try. (*thoughts*) Why did she say that? I'm done for.

CAROLINE: May I ask you a favour?

BRENDAN: Of course.

CAROLINE: In your speech would you be good enough to make some reference to my dear departed husband, Roger? How he'd have loved to be with us on this splendid day … that sort of thing.

BRENDAN: Certainly, Caroline. My pleasure. (*thoughts*) Oh God. Who? Roger. Roger. Roger.

MAURA: (*whisper*) Don't use the napkin to wipe your face.

SHEILA: Dad, pass the bubbly please. We're dying from thirst over here.

MARK: Let me ... (*sounds of cork popping, giggles and champagne being poured*)

BRENDAN: Who's that over there?

CAROLINE: That's our vicar,

BRENDAN: A vicar?

CAROLINE: Yes. Robin Derwent. A marvelous pastor.

BRENDAN: (*thoughts*) "Reverend Fathers, *Vicar*, ladies and gentlemen ... " No, not *Vicar*. "Reverend Fathers, *Padre...*" That doesn't sound right. What is it? Damn!

WAITRESS: Anyone for seconds here?

MAURA: I couldn't.

CAROLINE: No thank you. (*sound of glass being tapped*)

JIM: Hush everyone. Hush please for the best man.

SEVERAL VOICES: Sssh ... sssh.

CHARLIE: Ladies and gentlemen – and that includes all clerics present... (*laughter*) It is my very pleasant duty to make a start on the messages of congratulation. There are rather a lot of them. So with your indulgence I propose to read them out in small batches between dance sets. Then, after that we'll start on the speeches. One advantage of this proposal is that everything will seem funnier as we take more drink on board...

JIM: I think that's funny already. (*laughter*)

BRENDAN: (*thoughts*) I'll be near the end. Good ... no, *bad*. I'll have to wait for ages. "Reverend Fathers, Padre, ladies and gentlemen... When Sheila met Mark we knew…" No. Left something out. "This is a wonderful day…" No. It'll be later. "This *has been* a wonderful day." No. They'll think it's all over then. And *Roger*. God, what about him? Have to work him in somewhere…

CHARLIE: The next telegram, no, a fax, is from Mark's side. From Sue and Bob Rainey of Sussex. It reads, "Dear Sheila and Mark, heartfelt wishes on your great day. Remember, marriage is not just a word; it's a sentence. And there's no parole or time off for good behaviour." Very droll. (*laughter*)

BRENDAN: (*thoughts*) Smooth … oh a real smoothie. Public school training no doubt. Not a 'hum' or a 'haw' out of him. I'm out of my depth completely… (*sounds of band getting ready*)

CHARLIE: Ah, I see the band is setting up. We want everyone on the floor and then we'll do some more messages and make a start on the speeches. Take your partners. Sheila and Mark out first please. And no close dancing. Save that for the honeymoon. (*Laughter, sounds of chairs being scraped back. Band strikes up a dance number.*)

End of Scene Ten

SCENE ELEVEN

Interior. Hotel Function Room, band finishes a different dance tune. Sounds of guests returning to tables.

SHEILA: (*breathless*) Will you try some champers, Dad? It's terrific. And you paid for it.

BRENDAN: I'm all right as I am.

MARK: It's a fabulous reception, Mr. Canavan, thank you very much, Sir.

BRENDAN: My pleasure. (*sound of glass being tapped*)

CHARLIE: Ladies and gentlemen, now that the telexes and faxes are out of the way and we all need a little rest from dancing, I suggest we make a start on the speeches...

JIM: (*slurring*) Oh, no. Not the speeches. (*laughter*).

CHARLIE: 'Fraid so. Protocol demands it. It gives me great pleasure to call on the best man to say a few words – oh, that's me. (*applause and laughter*)
Friends, this is a truly wonderful day...

BRENDAN: (*thoughts*) That's my line! He's ruining me.

CHARLIE: I need to gather my thoughts. This is not too difficult; they don't range very far... (*laughter*)
You may or may not know that it was a rugby

injury that first brought Sheila and Mark together. For it was she who nursed him back to health and gave him sponge baths even when he didn't need them... (*laughter*)

When they started going out together he didn't talk about her the way he did about other 'conquests'. We all knew there was something serious in the air. Blokes can sense things like that. We've got intuition too… (*laughter*)

Naturally, when one bloke tells his mates he's thinking of tying the knot it's incumbent on the rest of us to talk him out of it. We don't like losing a member of our bachelor club. But Mark wouldn't listen. He had made that thing we all fear and dread … COMMITMENT. And he even mentioned that other terrifying word that drives strong men to drink … the L- word. (*laughter*)

Well, ladies and gentlemen, Mark and I knocked around together for years. We played rugby and we showered together…

Guests: *Ooooooh!*

CHARLIE: And I want to tell Sheila something about Mark if she doesn't know it already. He has a large … mole on his back… (*laughter*)

JIM: Are ye poofs or what? (*laughter*)

BRENDAN: (*thoughts*) He's good … can't follow that. Palpitations now. Am I going to pass out? Maybe all for the best…

CHARLIE: So in conclusion may I ask you to charge your glasses and join me in wishing long life and happiness to Sheila and Mark.

(*sounds of pouring, clinking glass, chairs being pushed back*)

GUESTS: Life … happiness … Sheila and Mark…

CHARLIE: Now how about another dance set and then we'll cut the cake and hear from Mark. (*Band strikes up.*)

End of Scene Eleven

SCENE TWELVE

Same interior.

CHARLIE: Mark, I thought you were a New Age man. The least you could do is help Sheila cut the cake.

MARK: I'm doing the best I can.

SHEILA: It looks too good to cut.

CHARLIE: Hold it there, like that, for a sec. We want a close-up on video. (*sounds of cake being cut and served*)

CAROLINE: (*mouth full*) This is delicious.

MAURA: Mmmm.

SHEILA: Mark, bigger portions.

MARK: But we have to keep some for the…

SHEILA: (*laughing*) Do as you're told.

MAURA: Good girl. Start as you mean to go on. Men need a firm hand.

CHARLIE: I now call on Mark to say a few words … if he's finished stuffing his face with cake. (*applause*)

MARK: Ladies and gentlemen, friends, I can't adequately describe what this day means to me. Most of what Charlie said was rubbish…

CHARLIE: Never! (*laughter*)

MARK: …But he got one thing right. After I first met Sheila I was a changed man… No longer a bloke. Of course I had to break my leg in three places to get to meet her but it was more than worth it…

WOMEN GUESTS: Aaaaah…

MARK: I was jolly well bowled over by her Irish charm and that certain … je ne sais quoi…

JIM: Ah, keep it clean now. (*laughter*)

MARK: I won't go on much longer because the most important speech will be from the father of the bride and we must conserve our powers of concentration for that. But I can't finish without thanking Father Joe, Sheila's parents and my mother who did such a good job with me… (*faint laughter*) Thank you also for the wonderful presents. Not one bathroom scales among them… (*faint laughter*) And now I'd like to propose the toast. To Sheila and family on both sides. (*sounds of glasses, drinking*)

GUESTS: Sheila … family…

CHARLIE: Ladies and gentlemen, I'm sure we're all greatly impressed by the oratory of the groom. Could I now suggest another dance set, after which we'll hear from the father of the bride. (*Band strikes up.*)

BRENDAN: (*thoughts*) "Reverend Padre, Roger, ladies and … a wonderful day when Sheila met Charlie…" No, no, no, no, no. Christ, what am I going to do?

JIM: Maura, how about a twirl?

MAURA: Why not?

JIM: Brendan, if you're not going to dance with

your glamorous wife, others will.
BRENDAN: What? Oh, right.

End of Scene Twelve

SCENE THIRTEEN

Same interior.

MAURA: (*breathless*) I'm worn out. Jim insisted on jiving. Still Great gas.

CAROLINE: (*breathless*) I can't remember when I had so much fun. I think that was a cousin of yours. He danced me off my feet.

MAURA: Paddy. Yes. He's a hoot. Never lost it. Brendan, you should give it a go.

BRENDAN: Maybe later. (*thoughts*) "Reverend Padre, wonderful day, welcome into family … Roger should be here…"

MAURA: (*whisper*) You should dance with Caroline. And you haven't danced with Sheila yet.

BRENDAN: Later. (*thoughts*) Doesn't she know I'm up next? Does she suspect anything? Christ, the best man is going to call on me anytime now. Notes wet with sweat … only one way out … can't … have to, no choice … drink. I'll have to have a drink … (*sound of pouring and drinking*)

MAURA: What're you doing?

BRENDAN: Nothing.

MAURA: But your pledge!

BRENDAN: Day that's in it. (*glugging sounds*)

MAURA: Well, if you must. But sip for God's sake,

don't glug. (*sounds of rapid drinking*)

BRENDAN: (*thoughts*) Get it down. Not much time. Could be called on any second. No way out.

MAURA: Brendan, for God's sake! Your first drink and you're turning into an alcoholic.

BRENDAN: So what? (*thoughts*) It helps. It does. Just a little more. (*sounds of drinking*)

SHEILA: (*returning to table*) This is an honour, Dad. Your first drink. On my wedding day.

MARK: Well done, Sir! Cheers!

BRENDAN: Good health. (*slurring*) I could get a taste for this stuff. (*drinks*)

MAURA: Brendan, remember you have your speech coming up.

BRENDAN: I haven't … forgotten.

SHEILA: Mark, time for another dance?

MARK: OK, but let me lead this time. OK?

SHEILA: Sure, snookums.

BRENDAN: (*thoughts*) Some more drink and maybe I'll be OK.

End of Scene Thirteen

SCENE FOURTEEN

Same interior. Background sounds of merriment now quite pronounced.

BRENDAN: (*drinking, thoughts*) I'm ready now. Great stuff. This champagne. Never so relaxed before ... Roger. Never met you. Don't know you from Adam. But I'll fit you in. Don't worry. Padre too. No problem. I'll wing it. Don't need these notes now. (*sound of tearing paper*)
(*thoughts*) Haven't a clue what I'm going to say and it doesn't matter. I'll be great. Off the cuff. Bring the house down. Show the Brits.

MAURA: Straighten your tie, Brendan. And put on your jacket. You're going to be called on any minute now.

BRENDAN: (*slurring*) Where's the best man when you need him?

MAURA: He's over there by the bandstand, talking into a mobile phone.

JIM: You OK now, Brendan?

BRENDAN: Yeah. Why wouldn't I be...? Where's Charlie now?

JIM: Over there. He's chatting with Mark.

BRENDAN: (*loudly*) Hey Charlie. Come on over here. (*thoughts*) I'm ready, boy. Got the monkey off my back at last ... vain. I'll give them vain. Talk up a storm. "Reverend Fathers, Padre, ladies and gentlemen … " To hell with that. "Hello everybody, are we having a good time? What? I didn't hear you. Are we having a good time? Are the happy couple going to have a great time tonight? You bet. Let's hear it for the happy couple…" They're all pissed anyway. Drink is a great leveller. How did I do without it all these years? Bloody pledge. Charlie, get your arse over here. By God, you're all going to get an earful. Bring on the video too. This is for posterity. The grandchildren are going to enjoy this… Ah, here he comes now. At last.

CHARLIE: Ladies and gentlemen, I've just been checking with the airport and the AA. There's a dreadful traffic problem. Sheila and Mark will have to rush to catch their flight. They've already gone upstairs to change. I'm afraid we won't have time to hear from the father of the bride. (*sounds of mock disappointment*) I'm sorry, Mr. Canavan. One of those things. It's very disappointing.

JIM: Oh, it is. It is.

CHARLIE: We should all go out to the lobby now to be ready to give the happy couple a good send off. (*sounds of guests leaving the function room*)

BRENDAN: (*thoughts*) No! No! I'm ready! Must say something. (*aloud*) Enjoy yourselves! Have a great time!

MAURA: (*stern whisper*) They've gone upstairs,

you eejit.

CAROLINE: Best speech of the day, Brendan. Short and to the point.

BRENDAN: But I want ... to say ... more.

MAURA: Thank God you can't. You're as tight as a tic.

BRENDAN: I'm entitled ... ent-it-led...

CHARLIE: Come on folks, everybody out to the lobby. We have to doctor the car as well before they come down. Sam, stand by with the videocam.

MAURA: Brendan, come on ... Brendan! (*sounds of snoring*)

MAURA: (*whisper*) God Almighty, he's passed out.

CAROLINE: Is he all right?

MAURA: Oh yes. Just a little tired, you know. (*thoughts*) Wait till I get you home. Just wait.

END

A GIFT

A Short Film

NOTES FOR ACTORS

A top scientist (the Professor) has given his dog (Thomas) the gift of human awareness by injecting him with genetic serum. Thomas is making a biopic of the Professor as an act of gratitude and also to record his scientific achievement for posterity.

The viewer does not know until the very end that Thomas (the narrator and cameraman) is, or was, a dog.

Thomas is very grateful to the Professor for the gift of awareness which he uses avidly to learn about life and about himself.

The Professor is embarrassed by Thomas's gratitude and by the film which is being made about him.

Towards the end of the story the Professor forgets to give Thomas his injection and when he returns to the house he is shocked to find that Thomas has reverted to being an ordinary, friendly pooch.

Tone: light and colourful at the beginning, more sombre towards the end.

Shooting: Hand-held camera effects. Thomas is behind the camera until close to the end.

OPENING OF FILM

1. INT … LARGE UNTIDY LOFT-STYLE APARTMENT … MORNING.

The camera picks out several wall mirrors, book-cases, dozens of books littering the floor, a microscope and PC on a desk. The camera moves to the sleeping section of the loft, picks out an empty bed (which Thomas has just vacated), rests briefly on a bedside table covered in mail and zooms in on a bearded man in another bed. He is beginning to wake up.

THOMAS
>   (*Off-screen, loud whisper*)
>   This is the Professor … teacher and mentor …
>   I'm proud to call him friend … *My* friend
>   believe it or not … I dreamed about him last
>   night…

THE PROFESSOR
>   (*Waking up, stretching*)
>   Morning, Thomas … (*Looks into camera*) …
>   Oh, the home movie … do we have to? Well, if
>   you must… Thanks for bringing up the mail.
>   But you don't have to do that, you know.

THOMAS

(*Off-screen*)
It's the least I can do… This film will show the world.

THE PROFESSOR
(*Shyly*)
Goodness me… Today is Saturday. Why don't we go out for breakfast?

THOMAS
(*Off-screen*)
Brilliant!

The Professor gets out of bed and starts to dress. He picks up a large photograph of a cat looking into a mirror, turns it around as he studies it.

THE PROFESSOR
No recognition. None at all.

THOMAS
(*Off-screen, sadly*)
Aaaah ……

2. EXT … SUNNY TREE-LINED SUBURBAN
   STREET … DAY

The Professor walks towards the camera, smiling shyly. He is clearly embarrassed by the film project but is prepared to do it for Thomas's sake.

THE PROFESSOR
Must we, Thomas…?

THOMAS
(*Off-screen*)
We must … (*Interior monologue*) There has to
be an archive. We're finite. You taught me that.

3. EXT … SAME STREET FURTHER ON …
DAY.

*A female neighbour, weighed down with grocery
bags, approaches.*

NEIGHBOUR
Morning Bill… Hi, Thomas … great day!

THOMAS
(*Off-screen, interior monologue*)
Professor to you, Missus. Show some respect.
He's a Nobel Laureate … and don't patronise
me.

*The neighbour nods goodbye to the Professor and
approaches Thomas with her hand out as if to give
him a pat. The camera begins to shake more than it
has done. The neighbour backs off and goes away.*

The camera becomes more steady, and picks out the entrance of the café they are going to. There are a couple of dogs at the entrance. The camera begins to shake again.

THOMAS
> (*Off-screen*)
> Oh Shit!

The Professor rushes to intervene.

THE PROFESSOR
> (*Urgently*)
> Down boy! Get away the pair of you … shoo!
> … Shoo!… No harm done, Thomas.

We see the dogs running away. The camera again picks out the café entrance.

4. INT … CAFÉ … DAY.

There are several mirrors on the walls of the café, which is decorated in the Art Deco style. The Professor is seated at a table and seems a little ill at ease. Other people are throwing curious glances at him and at the camera. A waitress brings two glasses of milk and two plates of toast. She gives a strange look into the camera and at Thomas.

THOMAS
(*Off-screen*)
Just toast. The Professor is a man of simple
tastes. Austere like all great innovators …
lovers of life, believers in a higher power…

THE PROFESSOR
(*Embarrassed*)
Easy on, old chap.

*The Professor drinks his milk. The camera lingers
over the wall mirrors again.*

5. INT … LIVING-ROOM PART OF LOFT-
   STYLE APARTMENT … EVENING.

*The Professor is reading and making notes. He
suddenly jumps out of his chair and knocks a text-
book to the floor.*

THE PROFESSOR
I forgot about the cultures … I have to go into
the lab, Thomas … I should be back before
midnight. Will you be all right?
(*He grabs a jacket from the back of a chair and
checks the pockets for his car keys. He
switches on the TV and throws the remote
control towards Thomas.*)

THOMAS
>(*Off-screen*)
>Go ahead. I'll be fine.
>*The Professor leaves the apartment and the*
>*camera picks out a Soap on the TV. It is a well*
>*known one. The camera begins to shake again.*
>(*Off-screen, interior monologue*)
>No real people in these soaps. Drivel. Not
>exactly a mirror held up to nature. (*Yawning*
>*sounds*) Nothing to learn from them ... no
>literary ... merit... (*More yawning sounds*)
>Switch off this garbage now... (*Deep,*
>*prolonged yawning sounds.*)

The TV screen goes blank. The hand-held camera
slips from Thomas's grasp and focuses on a wall
mirror. There are snoring sounds.

6. INT ... THE SAME ... NIGHT.

The mirror is still in shot but is now reflecting,
through a window of the apartment, a moonlit night
and lighted buildings.

THOMAS
>(*Off-screen, interior monologue*)
>Must have dozed off ... something wrong ...
>oh God, forgot the serum ... my fault ... old

smells coming back ... mice, snails... What's that...? Mo – oon, they call it ... words go first... That bitch next door ... coming on heat ... no good for me not since Vet ... no pups for Thomas... Dog years fly by ... inject ... in-light going ... go ... wo ... woo ... woof...

Sounds of dog barking.

7. EXT ... MOONLIT STREET ... NIGHT

(*More professional camera-work from this point on.*) *A taxi squeals to a halt. The Professor jumps out, enters his apartment block and runs up the stairs. He bursts into the apartment.*

8. INT ... LIVING ROOM PART OF LOFT-STYLE APARTMENT ... NIGHT.

The Professor rushes across the room.

THE PROFESSOR
Oh, Thomas, Thomas ... I forgot the injection ... I'm so sorry...

We see Thomas's small camera on the floor where it has fallen. The camera has a couple of

*special lever-like attachments. Then we see
Thomas for the first time. He is a red setter. He
is lying on the carpet and jumps up to greet the
Professor who kneels with him in an embrace.
There are tears in his eyes. He keeps looking
into the dog's eyes as if trying to interpret how
he is feeling.*

(*Crying*)
We were so close to perfection, Thomas, so
close … Can you forgive me? I raised your
hopes … I know it … (*He reaches for the
small camera.*) This distracted me… The least
I can do is destroy the tape … what do you
think…? No…? A walk … walkies…?

*Thomas frisks with him and licks his face. The
camera zooms in on the Professor's face and shows
that he is cheered up a little by the dog's affection.
The camera then slowly pulls away until Thomas
and the Professor form a small tableau in the middle
of the room.*

THE END

A CONVERSATION BETWEEN BETWEEN GEORGE ELIOT AND FREDERICK BURTON

Frederic William Burton (1816-1900)
Hellelil and Hildebrand, the Meeting on the Turret Stairs, 1864
Watercolour and gouache on paper, 95.5 x 60.8 cm
National Gallery of Ireland Collection
Photo © National Gallery of Ireland

NOTES FOR ACTORS

Sir Frederick William BURTON, an Irish painter and Director of The National Gallery of Britain, has carried a burden of guilt for many years. At last he has an opportunity of discussing it with his friend, George ELIOT, whose real name was Mary Ann Evans. Frederick calls her Marian. She calls him Frederick. Both of them have dedicated themselves to artistic integrity and they trust each other implicitly. The conversation ends with a discussion of his masterwork, *Meeting on the Turret Stairs*, a painting which was voted the best loved painting in the National Gallery of Ireland.

FREDERICK WILLIAM BURTON (FWB) *and*
GEORGE ELIOT (GE) *are seated in the living room
of his house.*

FWB: Did I tell you how much I enjoyed your latest
novels, Marian. 'Middlemarch' was
outstanding.

GE: Thank you, Frederick. I'm not sure if there is
any writing ability left in me. The years have
caught up. My husband is failing, as you know,
and I've moved out of London to care for him.

FWB: Age is insidious. It comes so quickly and
silently. I … we always think there is time to
do more … to leave a better legacy. But we can
so easily be deprived of that chance. Your
legacy, Marian, is more than secure. But mine
… I wonder?

GE: You need not worry about that, Frederick … I
meant to ask if your fiancée spoke to you after
she and I last met? She seemed to be rather
upset…

FWB: Really? Concerning what?

GE: You know, I'm not … really sure…

FWB: I'll talk to her … though she's probably
forgotten about it, whatever it was.

GE: Have you set the date for your nuptials yet?

FWB: Not an exact date … no…

GE: Perhaps it would … be wise to do so … an
exact date can reinforce an intention… I
apologise. I do not mean to interfere.

FWB: No, of course not… It is good advice … from

a friend who has our best interests at heart.

GE: Absolutely, Frederick. I would not have spoken from any other motive.

FWB: I know … and I will reflect seriously on your advice… (*Intense*) May I ask you something, Marian? I have been wrestling with an issue for a long time.

GE: Of course, Frederick. You may ask me anything.

FWB: Is it fair to say that your work does not concern itself primarily with social reform?

GE: That is fair. I do not campaign to change society, Frederick. My focus is mainly on individuals. If they work in Satanic Mills I sympathise with them, and will write about their travails. But I do not preach revolt against factories and mines – or society in general.

FWB: (*Pensive*) The reason I ask is because about twenty years ago I was painting Thomas Davis, a leader of the Young Ireland movement. He took me to task for not using my work to help resolve some of the dreadful social and political problems in Ireland. He made me think, and I developed a conscience about it – my passivity…

GE: Passivity? I doubt that, Frederick…

FWB: While I lived in Germany I often thought I was running away from my responsibilities. I still worry about it. Thomas Davis died young and didn't live to see the Young Irelander Rebellion, such as it was. But his words haunt me to this day.

GE: His cause was just … and he was a good poet who wrote for Everyman. Some might say it was too popular to be truly great. Maybe he could have written great poetry if he had not used it to preach to people, or to convey his political philosophy. Now we will never know.

FWB: I told him at the time that I did not want to engage in propaganda. But I now feel it was selfish on my part … especially after the horrors of the Great Famine which I never had the courage to engage with in my painting.

GE: I think you are too self-critical, Frederick. Art is art, not propaganda. A great novel never halted a cavalry charge. Art deals with the human heart, not with people *en masse*, nor with structures and institutions.

FWB: (*Awkward*) I still worry about it. Maybe one could have been a little more concerned with the issues of the day. After all, *you* learnt Hebrew to fight anti-Semitism…

GE: No, Frederick. I learnt Hebrew so I could understand the poetry of the psalms. Sometimes if you concentrate on truth it may well be at the expense of beauty. I have always been struck by the beauty in your work, especially 'The Meeting on the Turret Stairs'… (*The painting appears.*) I said before, when that painting first appeared, that the way Hildebrand kisses the arm of Hellelil is sacramental. You captured a moment of intense love and beauty. It will be an important part of your legacy.

FWB: (*Modest*) It took me forty-five sketches to get it right.

GE: That doesn't matter. You knew precisely what you wanted to achieve. You tried and tried again until your imagination was satisfied.

FWB: Well … possibly…

GE: You caught the essence of that myth. Everyone can now experience that moment because you have immortalised it. That is art at its best. You should not think it can go further and solve the practical problems of life. That cannot be its purpose.

FWB: No? You think not? I greatly value your opinion, Marian. But you must not be diplomatic…

GE: Diplomatic! Me? I don't think you need worry about that, Frederick … I was regarded as a dissenter and marriage-destroyer in England. No, the painting speaks for itself. The beauty of the moment is made even more intense by the pall of doom that surrounds the two figures.

FWB: (*Impressed*) You can see that?

GE: Yes, of course. The viewer sees immediately that their love will be forbidden and finally thwarted. We see that in the averted faces, in the tension of Hellelil's slender back and the way she has to support herself against the wall. We see it in the flowers she has dropped on the steps. We see it in the way her hair is trapped in the cinch around her waist. Those were not accidents, Frederick.

FWB: No, not accidents…

GE: They cannot look at each other. It is as if each of them already feels guilty for the awful destiny that awaits the other. Hildebrand's sword and helmet suggest that disaster lies ahead. We know that his chain-mail will not be enough to protect him … or her.

FWB: And the confined space of the turret…

GE: Yes. Yes. There is no possibility of escaping their destiny … We see looming disaster in their expressions. Beauty is often paradoxical. It can occur at moments of extreme tragedy. The Greeks knew this only too well… You have captured that tragic beauty in your painting … what more can you do?

FWB: I … sometimes wonder ……

GE: Of course you wonder and doubt yourself, Frederick. I sometimes think that artists in general have to be in conflict with themselves – perhaps unconsciously. I would hazard a guess that the choice of blue for Hellelil's dress is related in some way to the innocence of the Virgin Mary. Hildebrand's red tabard is no surprise, since red represents action.…

FWB: Yes … yes … exactly…

GE: What happens when red and blue are mixed together? You get the royal colour, the colour of power and influence. But we know that it can never happen in your painting because the lovers will be torn apart. They will never have power. Love will ruin them.

FWB: That was not intended … the mixture of colours, I mean…

GE: No. But it's there. And I warrant it is no coincidence. Art is not about power. It is about a lyrical moment when time seems to stand still. You could have painted the warring families behind this myth but you did not. You chose the most intense moment of the tragedy, the exact point where love, life and death intersect. No one could do more.

FWB: (*Relieved*) I hope you're right.

GE: I am right. Your province, Frederick, and mine, is the human heart, whether it resides in England, Ireland, or Germany. There are other more practical people who are better equipped to agitate for the reform of society…
(*She stands.*)
But we should always remember that if we can nourish the heart then maybe, just maybe, good conscience and good deeds can follow.
(*Beat*)

FWB: That would be wonderful…

GE: But you can't make it happen.

FWB: No … I see that now.

GE: May I ask *you* something, Frederick?

FWB: Of course.

GE: The moment of lyrical intensity in your painting … (*Diffidently, she looks closely at him.*) … it must have a special meaning … for you… Perhaps it was always … with you…?

FWB: (*Awkward*) I think … I may have carried that image … of perfection between two people … in my heart … all my life… Perhaps a sort of ideal that could never be realised…

GE: (*Gently*) A meeting of souls?

FWB: Yes…

> (*He stares at her and nods.*)
>
> Yes…

GE: You have given expression to it, Frederick. Be content with your special gift. Promise me?

FWB: I … promise … (*Beat*) … I am most grateful to you, Marian.

GE: I'm sorry you carried this burden of doubt … and guilt … for twenty years. I hope that maybe I have eased your mind a little, Frederick.

FWB: (*Smiles*) More than a little, Marian…

GE: At this time of life we should let go of our worries…

FWB: Yes … we should let them fly far away… Thank you, Marian.

> (*He stands and goes to kiss her hand. As he does so, she places her other hand on his paralysed arm in a gesture of affection.*)

Lights down.

END

THE FATTED CALF

Bartholomé Esteban Murillo (1517-1682)
The Return of the Prodigal Son, c.1660
Oil on canvas, 104.5 x 134.5 cm
National Gallery of Ireland Collection
Photo © National Gallery of Ireland

NOTES FOR ACTORS

MA and DA, late forties or early fifties, Dort accents. MA pronounces 'Dara' as 'Dawra', and 'Da' as 'Daw'. DARA, their son, nineteen, neutral accent, walks with a limp. He is a clone of his 'twin' brother, and his name means 'second' in Irish. CÉAD, twin son, nineteen, speaks like parents though with a London overlay. His name is pronounced 'kayd' and means 'first' in Irish. CÉAD is treated like the Prodigal Son.

All wear futuristic dress or accessories and carry tiny palm-pilot computers.

Both sons can be played by the same actor.

Interior, living quarters, large window gives a view of the sea. Modern cacophonous 'classical' music is playing. MA *and* DARA *are sitting at a breakfast table.*

MA: Dara, have you seen your Da this morning?

DARA: No. Why would I know where he is?

MA: Your eyes work all right … don't they? Ah, here he is at last with breakfast.
(DA *enters carrying a tray. He serves small glasses of compote. He sits. They sip from the glasses.*)

DARA: (*Rubs his stomach*) Not bad for once. This concoction almost hits the spot.

MA: This compote is delicious … halibut flavour with a hint of cinnamon. Dara, you could thank Da for making breakfast.

DA: Ah, it's all right, Ma. He's a … teenager. We were all like that once.

DARA: (*Meaningfully*) I don't think so … am I supposed to be grateful for something? Am I?
(*Awkward silence. Beat. Da looks around, stands, goes to window, returns.*)

DA: Cold as a witch's tit out there, and the sea is getting up.

DARA: That's something else they got wrong. Global warming me arse.

MA: (*Anxiously*) I wonder what time Céad will arrive today.

DARA: I won't lose any sleep if he doesn't get here at all!

DA: (*Troubled rather than angry*) Ah now, Dara, …
your … twin … brother.

DARA: Oh Yeah? Anyway, what does he want after
all this time? He's always on the make … I bet
he wants something. I can sense it.

MA: (*Annoyed*) Dara! Don't speak about your
brother Céad like that!

DA: (*Nervously*) It's kind of … understandable
though…
(*Da clears the table. Then he taps at his palm-
pilot and stares at the tiny screen*)

DA: Céad is on the hydroplane and is making good
time.

MA: Great … (*Anxiously*) Any word yet from his
doctor?

DA: No … nothing yet on his website.

DARA: (*Suspiciously*) Doctor? What doctor?
What's going on…?

MA: Dara, I hope you'll make an effort to be civil
when Céad gets here. Do it for Momma.
(*Dara lights up a joint.*)

MA: Dara how could you? Put that spliff out
immediately! Are you trying to … devalue
yourself?
(*Ma grabs the joint and extinguishes it.*)

DARA: Well, I can't compete with Céad … the
Golden Boy… But I know the score.
Remember that. I know the score!

DA: (*Nervously*) Steady on, son. This is … the
world we live in.

DARA: Yeah, and it was your generation that let it
happen.

MA: I wish you wouldn't talk to your Da like that. Why can't we all make the best of it?

(*Dara gets up, walks with a limp to an easy chair where he flops down.*)

DA: Is the pain still bad?

DARA: What do you think?

MA: I'm going to the Hydro-Port to meet Céad.

(*Ma checks her computer, puts on a coat and exits.*)

DARA: Make sure to carry his bags…

MA: (*Off*) We'll hire a robot.

DARA: (*More quietly*) I never get away, not even to England. I often look at the ships and hydro-planes on the horizon, but I know I'm not going anywhere. Not with this tag.

(*He raises his trouser-leg to reveal an electronic tag on his ankle.*)

DA: I know it's been tough on you… Let me see the wound…

(*While DA is walking towards him, DARA lifts up his shirt and surreptitiously removes a pistol from the front of his waistband and replaces it to the rear. DA, who has not seen the pistol, examines the wound.*)

DA: (*With forced optimism*) The stitches are nearly absorbed. Healing is well under way…

DARA: Yeah, but for how long? What's the point?

DA: (*Sadly*) Dara, you know my view. It should never have happened. But there was that European law and then the Church got in on the act…

DARA: I know you mean well, Da. But none of that

helps me.

(DA *pats him on the shoulder.*)

DA: Go up to bed and have a lie down. Here, have a couple of these babies.

(DA *hands him two pills.*)

DA: They'll help you chill… Don't tell Ma … I'll call you later.

(DA *links him out and returns. He tidies a bit and checks his palm-pilot.*)

DA: No news from the Doctor yet … that's something…

(*He hears a key in the door. MA and CÉAD enter. CÉAD looks exactly like DARA but is better dressed and has long hair. He moves with some difficulty but in a different way to CÉAD.*)

MA: (*Excitedly*) Look who's here! The wanderer returns…

(DA *embraces* CÉAD.)

DA: (*Excitedly*) Céad … great to see … long time, long time…

CÉAD: (*Making an effort*) Hi Da! You and Ma are looking fabuloso. This place really suits you. You should have moved out here years ago from the city.

DA: (*Scrutinising him*) You look a little tired, Céad … rough crossing?

CÉAD: Not really. The hydro-plane does it in an hour nowadays… How is Dara?

DA: Ah, he could be better I suppose…

CÉAD: Oh, yes, the … operation … but he's recovering right? He *is* recovering?

MA: (*Fussing over him*) Oh, he's fine, Céad. They do good work in the Hospital... Don't worry about Dara. He'll bounce back... Now, how about something to eat? Da got some nice mackerel-flavoured compote at the market...

CÉAD: That sounds great, Ma. But later, OK? I need to sort out a few things and have a shower...

MA: Of course, Dorling. Whatever you want to do. This is your home.

DA: (*Curiously*) Are you back for a holiday ... or ... did the doctor...?

MA: Not now, Da! Get his bags and bring them upstairs to the front bedroom.
(MA *accompanies them to the exit, rushes back, sits and switches on her palm-pilot.* DA *is carrying the bags. He and* CÉAD *exit.* CÉAD *walks slowly and appears stooped.*)

MA: Freshen up, Céad! And get some rest.
(MA *studies her palm-pilot with growing concern.*)
(DA *enters, studying his palm-pilot.*)

DA: (*Anxiously*) There's ... something ... being uploaded...
(*Beat*)

MA: Oh God in Heaven! It's worse than I thought...
(*She takes a pill.*)

DA: (*Shocked*) That message from his doctor. I can't believe it ... I thought Céad didn't look well ... But this...? I didn't think an infarction could cause...

MA: (*Distressed*) How do you think I feel? Jesus

mercy...

(DARA *enters, stands.*)

DARA: Céad wants something, doesn't he? Oh, Christ, I can tell from your faces. I gave a kidney last month. What does Céad want? An eye? A lung, maybe? A soul? Oh, no, I nearly forgot ... clones don't have souls...

(*Beat*)

DARA: (*Nervously*) What is it?

DA: Sit down, Son.

(DARA *limps to a chair and sits.*)

DARA: (*Aggressively*) What? What is it?

DA: (*Diffidently*) Céad has a rare form of cardiac infarction. His doctor is concerned...

(DARA *jumps to his feet.*)

DARA: (*Incredulous*) Cardiac ... heart? Heart? Are you mad? Have you lost it completely?

MA: He *must* have a transplant.

DARA: That's crazy! Do you know what you're saying?

MA: You have to be the donor, Dara. The tissue matches. That's not a concern ... you needn't worry about that...

DARA: (*Shouts*) That's not what I'm worried about ... this is *my* heart ... mine...

(DARA *thumps his chest.*)

MA: Aren't we being just a little ... possessive ... Dara?

DARA: *We're* not ... but *I* bloody well am... You got that right!

MA: Trust me. There won't be a problem of rejection...

DARA: (*Shouts*) I don't give a shit about that. I'm rejecting him … tell him to fuck off!

MA: Dara! You know I don't like that language…

DARA: Oh, you don't like that language?

MA: No, I don't. I'm your Momma… Look, you know how the system works… You don't own your heart…

DARA: Oh, I don't, do I not? Funny, that … It feels part of me…

MA: It's common property, Dara. You know that … don't give Momma a hard time…

DARA: Just because Céad came out of your womb and I didn't. Is that my fault? Is it? Clones are human too. We have rights…

MA: Not according to the Constitution. There would have to be a referendum.

DARA: (*Shouts*) Clones are not allowed vote!

MA: Do you really have to shout at Momma?

DARA: (*Heatedly*) And the Church says we've no souls. We have no legal protections … Da, what do you say?

DA: (*Conflicted*) The … cards are stacked, Son. At the beginning the scientists didn't think clones would have awareness… It was thought they'd be something like … well … sheep…

DARA: Sheep? Fucking sheep?

MA: Dara! I'm surprised at you! You're Momma's second favourite…

DA: It was a mistake … but there it is. The last clone who refused … was brought to hospital … and they harvested him by force…

DARA: That's murder!

DA: But the law doesn't agree… And the
government is exporting organs all over the
world … we all have to pay off the bank debts
of thirty years ago … I can't see a way out,
Son … I just can't…
(DA *bows his head.*)

DARA: Harvest the bloody bankers! They're the
ones who fucked up … pull out *their* giblets…

MA: You can't get blood out of a stone, Dara. It's
not on…

DA: I'm sorry, Son.

DARA: Why don't you donate *your* organs?

DA: Too old, Son. My organs aren't the best … I'm
told the liver is like a Swiss cheese.

DARA: That's your last word?
(DA *remains silent.*)

MA: We have to make the best of it… (*Beat, canny
appraisal of* DARA.) Actually … come to
think of it … your Da could do with a new
liver … and I could use a kidney.

DARA: (*Incredulous*) Wha-a-t? You want me to…?
You'd like to empty me out, is that it? Whip
out everything that's going? This is a great
family … I'm the gift that keeps on giving…

MA: We know it's not easy, Dara … Momma knows
that … but be reasonable…

DARA: Aw, fuck this!
(*He draws the gun and waves it around.*)

MA: Where did…? What the hell…?

DA: Shooting us won't solve anything, Son.

DARA: I can shoot Céad.

DA: No, you can't. You're made from his DNA. I

know you. You won't be able to do it. Give me the gun…

DARA: I've a better idea.

(DARA *points the gun to his own head.*)

DA: No!

MA: Don't do it. Don't! Give the gun to Momma… We're very fond of you, Son…

DARA: Oh Yeah? I'm worth more alive than dead! Isn't that what it's all about?

MA: Don't be selfish Dara. Think of others for a change. You used to be such a good boy.

DARA: (*Cannily*) Wait now… If I shoot myself, the harvesters could still get here in time … the organs would be usable … I've got a better idea.

(DARA *drops the gun on the table, rushes to the window.* DA *tries to catch him but is too late.* DARA *jumps out the window.*)

DA: Oh God! He jumped…!

(MA *rushes to the window, looks out and down.*)

MA: He's really done it now. Fell on the damn railings. Guts everywhere. Nothing left for anyone.

DA: The poor lad. He never had a chance.

MA: He aimed for those railings, the spiky ones … he did it out of spite … the selfish little brat… Of course he smoked and drank for years to damage his organs … to devalue himself… Still, I wonder if there's anything worth saving…

(CÉAD *enters.*)

145

CÉAD: I heard something. What's up?

MA: Look out the window.

CÉAD: Aaah shit! I knew he'd bottle it. My new heart is gone now. The bastard. What a goddamn waste. I'm done for ... what're we going to do now...?

DA: I don't know ... I just don't know...

MA: (*Thoughtfully*) But, that *is* a good question... What ... are ... we ... going to do ... now... (*All stand and stare at the gun on the table. They look at each other.*)

MA: (*With calculation*) You won't live without a heart, Céad ... That's a shame ... of course it is ... a real shame ... You're Momma's favourite... But your other organs are OK ... you never even smoked ... you looked after yourself, didn't you...? (MA *looks cannily at the other two and then at the gun on the table. The others do likewise. She advances slowly towards the gun, pretending to look elsewhere. The others do much the same.*)

MA: Waste not want not ... (*She lunges for the gun; so do the others.*)

CÉAD: (*Breathlessly*) No way! Get off...! (CÉAD *manages to grab the gun.*)

MA: Think of the family for a change...! Be a good boy...! Hand it over to Momma...! (*They all wrestle and jostle for the gun. At one point* CÉAD *holds it aloft. They all reach up for it.*)

CÉAD: Aaaggh! My heart...!

DA: Drop the gun, Céad!

CÉAD: No! No! Get away. My own parents…! I'm not the clone! I'm not the clone!

MA: It's for the best, Son … you're done for anyway. Give me the gun, Dorling…
(*The characters continue to fight strenuously and noisily for the gun with much improvisation. They pull and shove each other.*)

DA: Hand it over, Son…!

MA: (*Breathlessly*) You … used to be … a good boy … a little dote… Give Momma … the gun… Give Momma … the gun…!
(*All three turn their backs to the audience. MA and CÉAD are both holding the gun aloft. DA is trying unsuccessfully to grab it. The tableau is suddenly frozen. Lights down. At the same moment the gun goes off. No one knows who, if anyone, is shot.*)

END

A PACT

NOTES FOR ACTORS

AGATHA and CHRIS, an elderly couple, are seated at the kitchen table in their neat suburban home having tea. They are a respectable middle-class couple. AGATHA is the stronger, more decisive personality though CHRIS can defend himself when he has to. Before they make the pact they are free and easy with each other. After the pact they become more careful and conniving.

SCENE ONE

Both characters are seated on a sofa in the living room.

AGATHA: I didn't like that place one bit. What did you think of it, Chris?

CHRIS: Dire. But I hate those places anyway. Still, I suppose we'll have to keep looking.

AGATHA: I mean why do all the inmates keep rocking slowly in their chairs. To and fro, to and fro. What's all that about? They look like zombies.

CHRIS: Maybe it's to reassure themselves that they're still alive. The rhythm of the womb? I don't know, Agatha. We've been looking now for what – six months? – and still haven't found a decent nursing home for ourselves.

AGATHA: And that creep on the keyboard, playing all the 'golden-oldies' and trying to get everyone up to dance. 'Waltzie-waltzie-time' … what a patronising little shit he was. And the smell of puke and drool mixed with pine spray and Dettol. Aaaagh! Just awful.

CHRIS: There's no respect for old people in this country.

AGATHA: I know. Once the hair goes grey people look through you. It's like being a vagrant. And doctors don't care. If you drop dead in their surgeries it's no skin off their nose. They're not going to be blamed or struck off if an old biddy snuffs it in front of them… You know, I don't think I want to keep on looking at nursing homes. It's too depressing.

CHRIS: But you know, Agatha, we didn't choose our parents well. Three of them got early dementia. We have to go by the genes. I mean, I forgot my front door key yesterday…

AGATHA: Ah that's nothing. We all forget things.

CHRIS: Well … I don't know. And the kids have said they'd feel happier if we got into a home where we could be looked after. Barbara seems quite concerned.

AGATHA: Huh! I don't know about Barbara. I think she just wants us out of the way. She might have her eyes on the house too.

CHRIS: That's a terrible thing to say. Barbara isn't like that.

AGATHA: You can't see straight where she's concerned. Your first-born daughter. I get that. But she's a tough cookie. Face it.

CHRIS: She has a kind heart and means well.

AGATHA: Barbara could build a nest in your ear and rob it. You could never see that, you big softie.

CHRIS: Well, the kids all have responsibilities now.

AGATHA: They're focused on their own families … I don't blame them for that. I certainly don't want to be a burden on anyone. Not even Barbara.

CHRIS: Me neither.

AGATHA: (*Reflecting*) If someone is really senile
would they know it? Would it bother them?

CHRIS: I suppose they wouldn't be aware.

AGATHA: They wouldn't realise they were being
treated like crap.

CHRIS: The trouble is we're aware now. And we
know *now* that we would be badly treated later
on. And we also know that there's no
government regulation or control on those so-
called nursing homes.

AGATHA: Imagine being lifted up on one of those
crane things and being lowered onto the loo …
And then having your backside wiped. Jesus
Christ. No … never! I'd shoot myself first.

CHRIS: Me too. I've been thinking along the same
lines.

AGATHA: Are you serious?

CHRIS: Never more so. A Glock and a glass of
whiskey in the bedroom. Go out with a bang.

AGATHA: Absolutely. Leave a note saying, 'Fuck
'em all'.

CHRIS: I like it!

AGATHA: (*Surprised but enthusiastic*) So do I…
Suppose you had a gun and I had a gun … and
whenever one of us sees the other beginning to
go ga-ga, we just take 'em out?

CHRIS: Whack 'em?

AGATHA: Yes. When we're certain they're losing
it.

CHRIS: Absolutely certain. Then bang! Quick and
clean … count me in. I can trust you not to
shoot unless you have very good reason.

AGATHA: And I would trust you. It'll work … it
will … oh wait now.

CHRIS: What?

AGATHA: What about the one who's left alive.

CHRIS: Well if it's me, I think I'd do myself in soon
afterwards, certainly no more than a year later.
And I'd find a new home for Bertie if he's still
alive.

AGATHA: Or have him put down. He's beginning
to smell…

CHRIS: A new home if at all possible. He'd be a
great pet for … another family…
(*Chris turns aside to hide his emotions.*)

AGATHA: Well, OK … let's agree on that then. Oh
but wait … where are we going to get guns?

CHRIS: I know someone… It'll cost … but I reckon
I can get two functioning firearms for less than
the cost of one week in one of those nursing
homes. I'll go to the bank and draw out the
cash tomorrow.

AGATHA: This might be the best idea we ever had.
And you know what the real bonus is?

CHRIS: What?

AGATHA: We needn't look at any more of those
bloody nursing homes.

CHRIS: Thank God for that… But listen, not a word
to the kids.

AGATHA: No, this pact is just between you and me.
Hug on it?
(*They hug.*)

CHRIS: I'm going to take Bertie for his walk.

AGATHA: That bloody dog is molting all over my

furniture. And he puked on my rug least week.
Any chance you could lose him in the woods?
CHRIS: Not a chance. Bertie is a great little pal.

Lights Down.

SCENE TWO

CHRIS *is at the kitchen table reading the newspaper when* AGATHA *comes in from the garden, sits at the table and lays the secateurs aside.*

AGATHA: Any news?

CHRIS: Oh nothing much. Politicians tearing lumps out of each other as usual… Barbara phoned to say hello.

AGATHA: I bet she asked if we found a suitable home yet?

CHRIS: It sort of came up in conversation.

AGATHA: It just came up…? I bet it did.

CHRIS: Now, now, Agatha… By the way I have a surprise for you. Close your eyes and put out your hand.
(*He lifts up a box from under the table, takes out two guns and puts one in her outstretched hand. She opens her eyes and is a little shocked.*)

AGATHA: God, it's a cold, brutal looking thing. Ugghhhh.

CHRIS: Efficient though. They're both Hi-Point .45 pistols. Often used by drug barons. Glocks and these beauties are their weapons of choice.

AGATHA: And now pensioners.

CHRIS: Be careful. They're both loaded. But the safety catches are on. Here, let me show you.
(*He shows her how to use the gun.*)

CHRIS: Catch on … catch off. And you don't pull the trigger. You squeeze it gently.

AGATHA: It's got a good heft to it. Good balance.

CHRIS: You sound like a pro.

AGATHA: Maybe I am … What about holsters?

CHRIS: I couldn't get any holsters. I'm going to keep mine in the back of my waistband.

AGATHA: I'm going to keep mine in my little yellow shoulder bag.

(*They pour tea and look at the two guns on the table.*)

AGATHA: They're obscene things aren't they? But still … mesmerising in a … funny kind of way.

CHRIS: I know what you mean. But they have a certain purity too. I can't describe it. A kind of honesty. There's no hypocrisy about them, no humming and hawing, no dithering. They do a job simply and cleanly. Bang. That's it.

AGATHA: Especially when there are rules … like we have.

CHRIS: Maybe we should write down the rules so that the survivor won't be accused of murder afterwards.

AGATHA: Good idea. Our own little Geneva Convention. I don't want to be arrested by some fat copper with gravy on his shirt.

CHRIS: You're assuming you'll be the survivor. It could be me.

AGATHA: It could indeed. Although *I* didn't forget my door keys yesterday!

CHRIS: Hold on there. We can't go into this arrangement where one party has a bias against the second party.

AGATHA: No on course not. It's just a little joke.
We start from a level playing field … like
Russian roulette for the over sixties. It could
catch on. I'm feeling a kind of frisson
already…

(*He looks at her.*)

AGATHA: So here we are packing heat.

(*He puts his gun in his waist-band.*)

CHRIS: I'm heeled.

AGATHA: I hope you have the safety on in case you
shoot your ass off.

CHRIS: Don't worry about that… Do you feel lucky
today…?

(*Agatha fetches her yellow handbag, puts her
gun in it and hangs the bag on her shoulder.*)

AGATHA: Don't mess with me now… Funny, it
does give you a sense of security. The right to
bear arms shouldn't be sneezed at.

CHRIS: I feel … I don't know…

AGATHA: What?

CHRIS: Sort of self-conscious … that I might say
the wrong thing, you know?

AGATHA: Look, I'm not going to shoot you if you
mispronounce a word or forget what time it is.

CHRIS: Well. That's a relief. But remember, even if
you did act in haste, so to speak, you'd still
have to shoot yourself within a year.

AGATHA: Yes, that's a sobering thought. It'll keep
us honest.

CHRIS: So when does our new arrangement begin?

AGATHA: Why not right now?

CHRIS: I was half-hoping we might begin with a
little truce.

AGATHA: No. Better to start now … one-fifteen on
Tuesday, the seventh of … what month is it?

CHRIS: May … no, ah, ah, ah … March! Phew,
what a relief!

AGATHA: You nearly made my day, Punk… Stop
it! We mustn't joke. Otherwise it could be a
disaster.

CHRIS: No guns in bed though.

AGATHA: Agreed. We could have nightmares and
shoot each other. Anyway, we can hardly show
signs of dementia when we're asleep.

CHRIS: Has it occurred to you that both of us could
already be ga-ga and that is why we came up
with this scheme?

AGATHA: Oh don't go all philosophical on me.
We're still *compos mentis* and this is a good
scheme.

CHRIS: You're right as usual… Oh, another rule
occurs to me … there must be no defensive
shooting.

AGATHA: What does that mean?

CHRIS: Suppose I say something daft by accident
and suddenly realise you're going to shoot me,
I might shoot you first to save my own skin.
Pre-emptive defence. You see?

AGATHA: Yes. That would be wrong. I agree with
that rule. No pre-emptive defence. There are no
weapons of mass destruction.

CHRIS: Ouch, aaagh!

AGATHA: What?

CHRIS: I'm sitting on my butt.

AGATHA: So? You always sit on your butt. That's what most people sit on.

CHRIS: No, the butt of the gun.

AGATHA: Can't you fit it in a bit better … between your … in your builder's cleavage…

CHRIS: I'll try.

(*He wriggles a bit.*)

CHRIS: Yeah that's much better. Snug in fact.

Lights down.

SCENE THREE

The kitchen.

AGATHA: (*studying her laptop*) I can't imagine
Donald Trump will make a good President.

CHRIS: Donald who?

AGATHA: Are you serious?
(*She looks surreptitiously at her purse.*)

CHRIS: No … just joking … joking … Trump,
Trump, Trump! However doolally we get we'll
never forget that name.

AGATHA: Bertie peed on the rug this morning.
We'll have to think about having him put to
sleep.

CHRIS: Ah no. Poor Bertie. It's just a little kidney
problem. I'll get him some tablets from the Vet.

AGATHA: I wonder if he's gone beyond that?

CHRIS: Ah no. He just needs a little tune up. Just
like the rest of us. Maybe it's his prostrate…

AGATHA: What did you say?

CHRIS: About a tune-up?

AGATHA: No, after that.

CHRIS: About his prostrate?

AGATHA: His what?

CHRIS: His prostrate … (*Beat*) … oh no, I meant
prostate. Prostate.

AGATHA: Hmmmn … Do dogs have prostates?

CHRIS: I don't know … but that's not memory … I

never knew … We should Google it. Or ask
Barbara to do it. She's good at it.

AGATHA: Barbara called this morning.

CHRIS: Good. Any news?

AGATHA: She mentioned the nursing home again.
She and her husband reckon they've found a
good one, called Sunny Climes.

CHRIS: We visited that one! Don't you remember?
A mad woman swung her walking stick at me.
Nearly took the head off me.
(*His hand moves carefully to his waistband.*)

AGATHA: (*Carefully*) Oh yes … of course … I
remember now… It just goes to show how
unconcerned Barbara is. She always put herself
first.

CHRIS: You're being a little hard on her. I think she
just worries about us.

AGATHA: She does in her hat! She was always able
to manipulate you. Do you remember that time
she got money from you to go to that concert?

CHRIS: (*Carefully*) Money … yes … pop concert
wasn't it? Who was playing?

AGATHA: What?

CHRIS: Who was playing at the concert?

AGATHA: Oh, some damn group.

CHRIS: You don't remember do you?

AGATHA: Yes I do. I just don't want to give you
the satisfaction.

CHRIS: They were The Stewed Prunes…

AGATHA: Oh yes, The Stewed Prunes.

CHRIS: No they weren't. I made up that name…

AGATHA: I knew that. I was just playing along.

CHRIS: Well, don't do that. It could be a very
    dangerous thing to do… We must have another
    rule. Don't pretend to remember if you can't.
    We have to be honest or this won't work… For
    the record, the group was The Red Hot Chili
    Peppers.

AGATHA: It was … I knew that.

    (CHRIS *gives her a doubting look*.)

CHRIS: Oh did you now…?

    (CHRIS *stands and fetches his golf clubs*.)

CHRIS: I think I'll get in a couple of holes before
    the next shower.

AGATHA: It's hardly worth going to play two
    holes.

CHRIS: Oh yes it is. It's important to keep … ac …
    act … active…

AGATHA: Don't ask me along whatever you do.

CHRIS: You hate golf. Always did.

AGATHA: No, I didn't.

CHRIS: Oh for goodness sake…

    (CHRIS *exits*.)

SCENE FOUR

The Kitchen. Both are sitting at the table, drinking tea. They are both completely white-haired and frail-looking. It is four years later.

CHRIS: (*Reading newspaper*) I see that Trump's been impeached...

AGATHA: (*Vaguely*) Is that ... good or bad..?

CHRIS: You wouldn't have had to ask that question three years ago.

AGATHA: I'm testing *you*.

CHRIS: (*Sipping tea*) Aaaagh! There's no sugar in this tea.

AGATHA: I suppose it's my fault?
(CHRIS *stands and tries different presses looking for sugar.* AGATHA *watches him and places her yellow purse on the table.* CHRIS *returns and sits.*)

AGATHA: Did you not find the sugar?

CHRIS: I think we're out of it.

AGATHA: We have plenty and it's in the usual place. Where is that?
(*Surreptitiously she opens the zip of her purse. He notices.*)

CHRIS: I know. Don't worry about that.

AGATHA: It's in the press just under the cutlery drawer. But you didn't even try there.

CHRIS: Aaaah.. ... I know where it is.

AGATHA: Then why didn't you try that press?

CHRIS: Em … Because I was looking for different sugar.

AGATHA: What kind of sugar might that be?

CHRIS: Em … em … BROWN sugar…

AGATHA: Since when did you change to brown sugar?

CHRIS: I just took a sudden fancy. It's better for you anyway. Helps the bowels. And it's good to change.

AGATHA: I don't buy it… Stick to the rules.

CHRIS: (*Pointing to secateurs*) I see you were doing some gardening this morning.

AGATHA: Yes. Pruning shrubs mainly.

CHRIS: Which ones?

AGATHA: What?

CHRIS: Which shrubs?

AGATHA: Oh I see. It's like that is it? Well, I started with the Oleria…

CHRIS: And then?

AGATHA: The … Cotoneaster…

CHRIS: And then?

AGATHA: The … eh … em… Look, stop this. I will not be subjected to an examination.

CHRIS: What shrub was next?

AGATHA: Emm … eh … furze…

CHRIS: There's no furze in the garden.
(He reaches back to the gun in his waistband. She notices.)

AGATHA: This is daft!

CHRIS: Was it the Veronica by any chance and then the Fuschia?

AGATHA: (*Loudly*) How … what…?

CHRIS: I was looking out the bedroom window.

AGATHA: You were spying on me? How dare you!

CHRIS: You lost your footing in the flower bed on the left. And there were several shoots you failed to prune.

AGATHA: My God! I'd almost forgotten what a snivelling little sneak you are.

CHRIS: I also saw you put your yellow purse on the table. You were going to do it, weren't you? The first shot. You just couldn't wait, could you? I cancelled the insurance policy by the way.

AGATHA: You're such a smart little shit, aren't you?

CHRIS: Smarter than you. Though that wouldn't be hard.

AGATHA: Isn't it amazing how stupid you are when it comes to Barbara? She winds you around her little finger.

CHRIS: You're jealous of her! I always knew it. Mad jealous. Because Barbara and I had something special.

AGATHA: You're not just senile. You're fucking crazy!

CHRIS: How dare you! You're ten sandwiches short of a picnic.

AGATHA: If you're so smart how come you don't see your other little pet, Bertie?

CHRIS: What…? Where is he? What have you done…?

AGATHA: I had him put down this morning. How

about that? The filthy little pissmire. He won't
cock his leg over my furniture anymore.

CHRIS: What have you done, you hard-hearted…
Poor Bertie … the poor little guy…

AGATHA: I did what had to be done … He should
have been put down years ago…
(*She reaches for the yellow purse.*)

CHRIS: You crazy lunatic…! Don't … don't do
it…!
(*She grabs her gun and he quickly follows suit.
Lights down. Two loud almost simultaneous
gunshots with flashes. Groans. Silence.*)

END

CUPIDITY

Rutilio Manetti (1571-1639)
Victorious Love, c.1625
Oil on canvas, 178 x 122 cm
National Gallery of Ireland Collection
Photo © National Gallery of Ireland

NOTES FOR ACTORS

DESMOND, a Sex Therapist, forty-ish, not quite as he seems.

JIMMY, a farmer, forty-five plus, awkward and troubled.

EILEEN, his wife, thirty-ish, more attractive than her husband! She has secrets too.

All three are in a therapy setting.

DESMOND: (*Pause*) … Ahhh … ummmmm … I
    know it's hard, especially for you, Jimmy. This
    is your first session. But you really should try
    to be more … forthcoming. We've been …
    aam … going around in circles for the last
    forty minutes, if I may say so.

JIMMY: Sure, I'm OK, Doctor. There's nothin'
    wrong with me. Divil a bit. But herself insisted
    I come along here today … to waste everyone's
    time…

EILEEN: Doctor, now you can see what I have to
    deal with. Complete denial … and sheer
    stubbornness…

DESMOND: Jimmy, I know you don't want to
    divorce Eileen, but…

JIMMY: I told you. There's no need at all for a
    divorce … Doctor … None … The Monsignor
    is dead-set against that anyway…

DESMOND: The Monsignor…?

JIMMY: Of the parish… He has very strong views
    on things like that. What God has put together
    … marriage is a sacrament, you know.

DESMOND: I see … I see … Jimmy, let me repeat
    that everything said here remains here. It is
    highly confidential. And there's no need to feel
    embarrassed. (*Beat*) You know, Jimmy,
    sometimes we men are reluctant to talk about
    … emotional problems that might lead to …
    certain dysfunctional … physical …
    inability…

JIMMY: (*Defensively*) I don't know anything about that class of thing. There's nothing wrong with me. I'm in good working order.

EILEEN: Oh for goodness sake … would you listen to that?

DESMOND: What I mean, Jimmy, is … have you ever considered medication … like Viagra…

JIMMY: Mother of God! Don't need that stuff … Jays…

EILEEN: You could try it … once in a while.

DESMOND: You see, Jimmy, what Eileen is really talking about is intimacy. She wants to be closer.

JIMMY: No she doesn't. Not with me anyway.

DESMOND: No? Hold it there, Jimmy … why would you say that?

JIMMY: She blames *me* for everything … (*Beat*) She's been coming here for ages. Probably givin' me down the banks… But did she tell you about *her* problem? I bet she didn't.

DESMOND: *Her* problem? Eileen … em … would you care to respond?

EILEEN: I haven't a clue what he's on about. I don't have a problem.

JIMMY: Oh you're perfect, are you? What about the car?

EILEEN: (*Loudly*) That's my business! Anyway, what's that got to do with … anything…?

DESMOND: Em … it just might be relevant … what about the car, Eileen?

EILEEN: I got a car a year ago, Doctor … I spend some time on it. So what?

JIMMY: You're always at it. When you're not driving it around, you're washing it, touching it up…

EILEEN: It's a grand little car for running around in.

JIMMY: It's only a Ford Focus, for God's sake … silver … two previous owners.

EILEEN: (*Annoyed.*) Not silver! Metallic oyster…!

DESMOND: Wait now, Eileen … mm … how much time per day would you spend with the car?

EILEEN: A few hours maybe … that's not the point…

JIMMY: At least six hours a day! She kisses the upholstery…

EILEEN: Well I … it's leather … cream leather!

JIMMY: She washes it in the barn every day. And when she gets it all soapy she drapes herself over the bonnet and slurps up the lather. She slobbers all over that car. Sometimes she puts her … bosooms up on the windscreen… It's not right … not right at all, at all… (*Beat*)

DESMOND: Hmmmm, I see … I see… There is a condition called objectum-sexuality. There's a well-documented case of a woman who had an affair with the Eiffel Tower … married it I believe… One recalls a case of a farmer who had a fling with a tractor… (*Beat*) And of course men sometimes love land … mmmmm … but a women and cars … that's rather unusual.

(*Desmond walks around ruminating.*)

JIMMY: So it's not my problem at all. Sure, how could I compete with a Ford Focus?

EILEEN: That's beside the point … maybe you
drove me to the car. Ever think of that?

JIMMY: It *has* to be my fault doesn't it? Yeah, I
made you have it off with a Ford Focus.

DESMOND: Hmmmm … yes, I see … I see … I
might suggest behavioural therapy for you,
Eileen. We can come back to that … But we
should talk about you, Jimmy. I presume it
would help your relationship if Eileen … tried
to give up the Ford Escort…

EILEEN: (*Upset*) Focus! Focus!

DESMOND: Sorry! Ford Focus … if she gave that
up and became a more … conventional …
wife.

JIMMY: Well that would help … I'm not a proud
man, Doctor. But it's hard when you're second
fiddle to a car with two previous owners. It's
not right … I'm not going to have any kids the
way this is going … no one to inherit the land
… three hundred acres of fine pasture.

DESMOND: (*Dreamily*) Three … hundred …
acres…

EILEEN: Don't be fooled by him, Doctor. He …
went off me long before the car came into my
life. Ask him what turns *him* on. He's out there
in the haggart for hours on end…

DESMOND: Jimmy, you've heard what Eileen said.
She thinks you have another interest.
Something that excludes her. You have to be
honest or we can't make any progress.

JIMMY: I suppose … I spend time on the computer
like … the odd … what do they call it…? Chat

room…?

EILEEN: That's not it! Do you take me for an eejit?

DESMOND: Honesty, Jimmy. Emotional honesty. It's for your own good. Believe me.

EILEEN: I've seen you out in the haggart with … with… Here's a clue … it's not human…
(*Beat*)

DESMOND: (*Clears throat*) I see… If it's … am … a … a … farm animal, Jimmy, that's all right. I've come across that before. It's not as rare as you might think. It's surprisingly common in Kildare, around the Curragh.

JIMMY: I don't know what ye're talking about…

EILEEN: Spit it out or I will…!

JIMMY: This is mad! Do you see now, Doctor, what I've to put up with?

EILEEN: It's not sheep, Jimmy. Oh no, that'd be too ordinary for you. Do you know what it is, Doctor?

JIMMY: Don't! Don't say anything! Don't!

EILEEN: Geese!

DESMOND: Geese…? Geese, you say?

EILEEN: Oh, yes.

DESMOND: I see. (*Swallows hard*) Aaam … well, there are some precedents … this was known in China during the Ming Dynasty. At the crucial moment of … am … ecstasy, the man would wring the neck of the unfortunate fowl, so as to … accentuate the…

JIMMY: (*Holding his ears.*) Aaaagghhh! Stop it! Shut up! You don't understand. It's not geese … it's a special goose … a wonderful goose …

Giddy … Giddy … is her name…

(*He begins to sob.* DESMOND *passes him a box of tissues. He uses one.*)

DESMOND: How are you feeling right now, Jimmy?

(JIMMY *takes out his own large handkerchief from his pocket. Some goose feathers fall from it to the floor.*)

JIMMY: (*Blowing nose loudly*) How do you think I feel? … terrible … terrible … like shite…

DESMOND: Am I to understand, Jimmy, that it's not just physical, that you have feelings for this … goose?

JIMMY: (*Passionately*) Giddy … she has a name … yes … yes … yes! If you must know … I … I killed the gander … He attacked me first … bit me on the arse … I had to kill him … he never respected her … Giddy was too good for him … Giddy … My Giddy…

(*Some more goose feathers flutter to the floor.*)

EILEEN: Oh my God! It's worse than I thought. You see now, Doctor, why I want a divorce?

JIMMY: No divorce … never … the Monsignor … the parish … wagging tongues … never!

EILEEN: What if the Monsignor heard about your goose?

JIMMY: He wouldn't believe it. You've no proof. Everything in here is confidential … you said so…

(JIMMY *guiltily picks up the goose feathers and strokes them lovingly. Beat. Desmond stands.*)

DESMOND: I know this has been traumatic for you both. But the issues are now out on the table … A Ford Focus and a goose called Giddy. Unfortunately, our time is up for today… But I want you to think about the following scenario. What if you, Eileen, phased out the car, and you, Jimmy, tried to do the same with the goose … am … Giddy … would that be the basis for rebuilding your relationship? I want you to think carefully about that for next week. All right?

EILEEN: Yes, Doctor. Thank you.

JIMMY: (*Mumbles*) Yeah … I suppose … yeah… Thanks…

> (*They shake hands. After shaking hands with Jimmy, Desmond wipes his hand on his trouser-leg.* JIMMY *and* EILEEN *exit.* DESMOND *fiddles with a tape-recorder.* EILEEN *then returns, moving quickly towards* DESMOND.)

EILEEN: (*Excitedly*) Did you get all that?

DESMOND: Oh yes. Loud and clear. (*He shows* EILEEN *the tape recorder, chuckles.*) We got it out of him … *eventually* … for a while there, the goose was … the elephant in the room…

EILEEN: If I threaten to let the Monsignor hear that tape, Jimmy will agree to the divorce.

DESMOND: (*Gushing*) That's absolutely wonderful … you'll get the farm as well … the land … mnnn…

EILEEN: Who cares about land as long as that man's goose is well and truly cooked.

(*She stamps on some of the goose feathers.*)
(*They embrace.*)
EILEEN: (*Reluctantly breaking free*) I have to go…
  Oh I'm so sorry, sweetheart … I must away…
DESMOND: See you tonight, My Pet?
EILEEN: In the Ford Focus.
DESMOND: (*Smiling*) Where else? I can't wait. It's
  wonderful to be part of this threesome. That
  cream upholstery and you, Amore Mio …
  vroooom, vroooom…
EILEEN: Oh, don't say that… Mmmnnnnn … You
  know how it gets me going … Till tonight, My
  Doctor of Love … in my Ford Focus of
  Love…
  (*They reach out operatically towards each
  other, blow kisses. EILEEN backs away then
  exits with a dancing skip in her step.*)

Lights down.

END

DIMPLES AND SIN

after Domenichino (1581-1641)
The Expulsion of Adam and Eve, 18th Century
Oil on canvas, 123 x 175 cm
National Gallery of Ireland Collection
Photo © National Gallery of Ireland

NOTES FOR ACTORS

Having been expelled from the Garden of Eden, ADAM and EVE are eking out a miserable existence in a damp cave in a part of the world surprisingly close to a river which, thousands of years later, will be called 'Liffey'. They speak with slight Dublin accents and are full of regret and recrimination. ADAM is squatting on the floor and is poking at some nuts and berries.

(EVE *enters from another part of the cave.*)

EVE: ...They're gone asleep at last...
ADAM: Who?
EVE: Who do you think? The boys... (*She jerks her thumb towards a corner of the cave.*) How many other people do you know in this cave ... or in the world for that matter?
(EVE *flops down beside him*)
ADAM: Ah ... always the bitter word...! (*He pokes at his 'food'.*) Is this it?
EVE: What?
ADAM: Nuts and things. Is this the dinner?
EVE: Yes. What did you expect?
ADAM: It's fierce ... bleedin' nuts again.
EVE: Shut your hole... If you knew how long it took me to gather them today ... as well as the berries ... the hands are scratched off me...
ADAM: (*Sighs loudly*) Aw God ... there's a worm in this berry...
EVE: Stop complaining. It's good for you.
ADAM: And this place ... it's such a kip ... everything ... is just a load of shite...
EVE: What's wrong now?
ADAM: You know well...
EVE: Oh not all that again, about being kicked out of the garden... Lookit, I suffered too...!
ADAM: We had it good in there. It was Paradise ... manna, honeydew, ambrosia ... lovely weather... None of this damn rain and fog... We were able to go around in our pelts ... swimming in lakes ... riding on unicorns...

Not freezing our arses off in this dirty oul cave.
(*He looks sadly at the projected painting.*)

EVE: (*Sarcastically*) And remind me again …
whose fault was it that we got expelled from
the garden?

ADAM: You know well … stop rising me.

EVE: Oh, I've forgotten… Was it my fault by any
chance…? Could it possibly have been *my*
fault?

ADAM: (*Thumps his chest.*) *I* didn't pick the apple,
did I? I didn't go near the tree of knowledge.
God said it was off-limits and that was good
enough for me… He's the Gaffer…

EVE: Yeah, but you took a bite…

ADAM: Just to take the bare look off you … I
wouldn't mind but it tasted terrible…

EVE: It was a cooking apple … how was I to know?
The serpent told me it would be real sweet. …
sweeter than honey, he said.

ADAM: And *he'd* tell you the truth, wouldn't he?
The devil … Satan himself… *He* said that sex
would be great too…

EVE: It might be if you knew how to do it … (*Beat*)
… I can't believe you still blame me after all
this time…

ADAM: You shouldn't have listened to the serpent.
He conned you with flattery. You fell for his
oul guff … "Oh Eve, you're lookin' great,
you're like an Angel, give us a kiss." … I never
trusted him … whenever he came near *me* I
told him to feck off out of it … I stood on his
neck once…

EVE: Oh yeah, you always did the right thing …
everything was my fault, wasn't it?

ADAM: Well, you didn't make it easy for me. (*Rubs
a rib.*) Aaaaah! Still sore here after all these
years…

EVE: So, I came from your rib … that doesn't mean
I'm less than you … or that I'm in the wrong.

ADAM: God wanted me to have a helpmate, a
companion to soothe my brow, to make life
easier for me… He told me I'd have one great
advantage…

EVE: What was that?

ADAM: There'd be no mother-in-law … I don't
rightly know what he meant… Anyhow, you
were created to look after *my* needs, not to
bugger everything up.

EVE: (*Loudly*) How dare you!

ADAM: (*Pushing the nuts away*) You invented sin!

EVE: I what? What did you just say?

ADAM: You heard me. There was no sin before you
came along …now we're all in deep shit.

EVE: Did it ever occur to you that the Gaffer set us
up?
(ADAM *jumps up.*)

ADAM: (*Shocked*) Don't say that about God… Are
you mad, Woman? Take that back
immediately!

EVE: What more can he do to us?

ADAM: You don't know, do you? He's all-powerful.
He can do anything.

EVE: Do you know what he said to me when we
were being thrown out of the garden?

ADAM: What?

EVE: He said "I will make your pains in childbearing very severe." Then he said, "Your husband will rule over you."

ADAM: (*Dreamily*) Rule over you … proper order. Spot on… Lookit, you're the first woman … you should set an example for any others who might come after…

EVE: It was a terrible thing to say… He was right about one thing though … the birth pains were fierce … I thought I was going to burst … and you weren't much help…

ADAM: Don't talk to me about birth pains. What about my rib? Still sore as hell… Anyway, I cut the cords … funny, the little dimples they left in the lads' bellies… *We* don't have dimples…

EVE: We weren't born in wombs, thicko… But you can forget that bit about ruling over me. No one rules over me … not even himself…

ADAM: I'd be more careful if I were you … he sees and hears everything.

EVE: You're such a coward, do you know that? Always were…

ADAM: Not cowardice. No. Love of God. Respect … *you* never had that.

EVE: I was just an afterthought to him. You were his favourite.

ADAM: Oh, poor you, boohoo, sob, sob… Lookit, I worked hard to do His will…

EVE: Didn't I hear you often enough…? "Yes, God … No, God … three bags full God… Is this fig leaf doing the job … am I modest enough…?"

You were sucking up all the time … tryin' to
become an angel … Fat chance of that…

ADAM: It's called respect. I was showing the man
respect. He can read our minds anyway. He's
all-knowing…

EVE: He doesn't understand women.

ADAM: How can you say that? He can see into
everyone's mind.

EVE: Well he can't read my mind…

ADAM: That's because you change it all the time.

EVE: I do no such thing … (*Beat*) … and even if I
did there'd be a good reason for it.

ADAM: Look, he made you in his own image and
likeness.

EVE: I'm me own person … *me*… I'm going asleep
now. (*She turns sideways.*) Imagine, we have to
sleep in the same bloody spot…

ADAM: (*Hopefully*) Eh … Eve … I suppose there's
no chance … you know … of … anything …
there's nothing going like…? (*He gives her a
poke with his elbow.*)

EVE: (*Withering look*) No chance. You're right for
once … you can rule over yourself.
(*Eve turns her back to him. Lights go dim. He
wriggles around for a while.*)

ADAM: (*Grumbling*) I can't sleep now … there's
nuts or shells sticking in me back…

EVE: Count unicorns.

ADAM: That's no good … I'm too het up or
somethin' … I need some sort of relief, like …
I dunno … something…

EVE: Go asleep!

ADAM: I can't … no good … I'll never … too …
toooo … (*He starts to snore loudly.*)

EVE: Oh, God, listen to that… (*She wriggles
around.*)
(*She goes to sleep. Lights down for a while.
Snoring stops. Silence for five beats. Adam
suddenly sits up. Lights come up a little.*)

ADAM: (*Loudly*) Eve! Eve!

EVE: (*Wakes and sits up*) What? What is it…?

ADAM: Angel … an angel!

EVE: What're you trying to say…? You think I'm
an angel? First thing in the morning? (*She
smooths down her hair and looks at the
projected painting.*) I was, once…

ADAM: No, no, no. An angel is after appearing to
me … in a dream … an angel…

EVE: A real angel…?

ADAM: (*He grabs her by the arm*) Yes … the Arch-
Angel Michael… With a message … a
message…

EVE: A message about what?

ADAM: A wonderful message, Eve … you won't
believe it…

EVE: Tell me.

ADAM: Eve … it's like this … God will give us one
more chance…

EVE: A chance for what?

ADAM: A chance to go back to Eden…

EVE: You're jokin'… Lookit, that's not even funny.

ADAM: No. It's true. Oh Eve, isn't it wonderful…
As long as we don't sin anymore. He's
forgiven you for the apple and for what you

were saying last night... He was going to send down a son to forgive us ... but the Angel said that sounded a bit complicated ... why not just forgive us, himself ... straight off, like...

EVE: And...?

ADAM: God decided to forgive us ... straight off. ... I can't believe it...

EVE: That Angel, Michael, always had a good head on his shoulders...

ADAM: But we'll have to be on our best behaviour from now on. No more sin of any kind. By anyone ... none.

EVE: You mean me? You can do no wrong of course. *You* should be careful. Pride is a sin.

ADAM: (*Excited*) I will be careful, I promise. We must all be very careful. Every member of the family ... everybody... (*Looks around the cave.*) Where are the lads?

EVE: I suppose they went out to play early....

ADAM: Isn't it fantastic news, Eve?... We can all go back to that fabulous place forever, for all eternity... Everyone who comes after us too ... it's just brill.....

EVE: We can leave this ... rat-hole. (*Excited*) There's a lot to do ... I'll have to go down to the river to wash me hair, and make the boys have a bath, and...

ADAM: Isn't it wonderful, Eve...? We'll all have to be on our best behaviour. And that includes the lads. Our very best behaviour ... I'm goin' to stop complaining for a start, and...

(*Noises off: "Stop it! Don't ... get off me!*

Ouch! Ah! Ah!")

EVE: What's going on out there?

ADAM: (*Looking to the mouth of the cave.*) It's just the two lads, playing…

EVE: It sounds serious. Maybe you should go out … There might be sin involved … it could throw a spanner in the works…

ADAM: Naw, it's just a play-fight … Cain is pretending to hit Abel with a club… What a great sense of humour those lads have … I'm really proud of them … God will enjoy their company… You know, Eve, when we get back to Paradise we should stop fighting among ourselves…

EVE: I agree … it's this place has me driven demented.

ADAM: Me too… But we'll soon be on the pig's back … for all eternity … everyone else too… Just think about that…

(*He hugs her.*)

(*Very loud thump and scream from outside. A blood-spattered club is thrown into the cave. Adam lifts it up and holds it above his head. He and Eve look up with fear in their eyes.*)

ADAM: Oh, God…!!!

EVE and ADAM: (*Simultaneously*) Nooooo!!

Lights down. Spotlight picks out the painting.

END

GET DOWN WITH THE GROOVE

NOTES FOR ACTORS

MUNGO and NAOMI meet in a night-club and though totally incompatible, they seem to have a good time. The reason is revealed towards the end.

A disco. Strobe lights and background music. Revellers are dancing on stage to the sound of Spencer Davis Group's 'Gimme some lovin'.

(MUNGO *enters at a point in the song 'So glad you made it' and starts singing along with the lyrics.*)

MUNGO: Gimme some lovin' every day…
　　　　(*The music continues at a lower level.*
　　　　MUNGO *eyes the girls, as he taps hands and feet to the beat. In a far corner* NAOMI *stands in an elegant dress.* MUNGO *looks around at his 'friends' seated at the table.*)
　　　　Not a bad spot this, lads. Wha'? Plenty o' little ravers over there in that corner…
　　　　(*He peers through the gloomy interior.*)
　　　　See yer wan there in the spotty frock…? All your good lovin' right Babe… Here, I'm gonna throw the shape at that wan… Watch me dust…
　　　　(*He pretends to lasso her and pull her in. He saunters over in a pimpstride and stands behind her, looking her up and down. He bumps his hip against hers.*)
　　　　Let's bop, Babe.
NAOMI: (*Turning, posh accent*) O, my gawd … ahm … ahm … I don't think so.
MUNGO: (*Annoyed*) What're ye doin' here so?
NAOMI: Slumming. What else?
MUNGO: Slummin'…? A posh tart … forget it so.
　　　　It's your loss … (*He turns to leave.*)

NAOMI: (*Sarcastically*) What excuse are you going to give your friends over there … after you've done the walk of shame?

MUNGO: No bother to me, Babe … I'll tell 'em you didn't look so good up close … spots … bad breath … a wart on your hooter… Look it's no skin off my teeth … I mightn't tell 'em anything.

NAOMI: Oh, all right then. I suppose one dance won't kill me.

MUNGO: (*Disguising relief*) Don't do me any favours, Babe. OK then … but leave the handbag there on the counter. I'm not dancin' around a bleedin' bag on the floor.

(*The music volume increases as* MUNGO *and* NAOMI *move onto the dance floor and falls again after a few beats. They dance vigorously. Both are good movers. He takes his jacket off, twirls it and flings it towards the table where he was seated.*)

NAOMI: (*Sarcastically*) Nice moves!

MUNGO: We got rhythm up in Ballyer… Not too bad yourself. Let me guess … Rathgar … Ranelagh…?

NAOMI: Killiney, actually.

MUNGO: (*Executing a difficult move*) Jaysis, way out there in the sticks. Past the Noggin, innit? (*He dodges someone's elbow.*) Hey, watch it, Chief! (*Ducks around behind Naomi*) Good few muck savages in tonight… Well what do you do for a crust? Air hostess or somethin'?

NAOMI: (*Patting coiffure*) Heavens, no. Do you

really see me serving tea to all those
Neanderthals going to Torremolinas? Oeuffff
… I don't really *do* anything – apart from
looking after the horses … thoroughbreds.

MUNGO: (*Wiping forehead*) Muckin' out stables an'
that … shovellin' shite with the boggers?

NAOMI: Hardly … supervising the grooms.
Exercising them … the horses I mean … not
the grooms.

MUNGO: Not short of the readies, then, wha'?

NAOMI: I get by.

MUNGO: Flaunt it when you got it, wha'? I like tha'
in a Babe.

NAOMI: I'm not a Babe by the way.

MUNGO: Not a *baby* babe. No … more a tarted-up
Babe … term of endearment, innit?

NAOMI: I see… And what is it that *you* do … for a
living?

MUNGO: (*Short of breath*) This an' that …
insurance mostly. Yeah, tha's it … I insure
people, knowarIme-an…?

NAOMI: Insure them against what? Fire and flood?
Acts of Gawd?

MUNGO: (*With a grin*) No … I insure them against
me … gerrit?
(*He makes a few karate moves and a high
kick.*)
Yeah, I'm the big risk…

NAOMI: Do *I* need protection from you?

MUNGO (*Taps his wallet*) No. I got plenty. Ribbed
and plain. Trojans and Commandos. Take your
pick … Luv.

NAOMI: You're very sure of yourself.

MUNGO: Why not? I like posh tarts. And you like a bit o' rough. I can tell … I've been around … (*He pinches her*). Mungo Steele knows the score a'righ'…

NAOMI: Mangow Steele?

MUNGO: At your service… And your handle, Babe?

NAOMI: Naomi…

MUNGO: Like that model mot? Good one. I like it … it has a ring to it … Nomio…
(*Lights come up a little.*)
How about a gargle, Nomio?

NAOMI: (*Not convincingly*) I'm with a party.

MUNGO: (*Wiping face and stroking back greasy hair*) A party? Those mots over there? Don't mind them … they know the scene. Come on.
(*He takes her by the hand and leads her over to the bar where he signals for service.*)
Hit me twice, Freddy, and put it on the slate. (*To Naomi*) They know me here. They're clients, like.

NAOMI: Clients?

MUNGO: Insurance, remember? Yeah, after a little persuasion, they took out a de Luxe Mungo Steele insurance policy, knowarIme-an? All risks included … especially me… (*He sips his drink*) Aaaaah, just the job.

NAOMI: (*Sips and shudders*) What *is* this? Rocket fuel?

MUNGO: Speciality of the house. Rum … an surgical spirit to kill the germs. Get it down …

it'll put hair on your chest…

NAOMI: (*Sarcastically*) You're very forceful, aren't you, Mangow?

MUNGO: (*Oblivious of sarcasm*) Babes need that … a firm hand. They don't like to admit it … but they need it deep down, knowarIme-an? Yeah, a firm hand.

(*He lights a reefer and throws the match over his shoulder.*)

NAOMI: Must you … smoke?

MUNGO: I must. I must. Me clients here don't object. What's the problem anyhow? Get real, Babe.

NAOMI: Reality isn't all it's cracked up to be.

MUNGO: You're up-tight, Luv … loosen up … wha's wrong anyhow? Hormones acting up? Maybe it's the curse, or whatever youse mots call it out in Killiney…

NAOMI: I don't have to listen to this cawdology! You're a chauvinist pig. You think women have hormones instead of minds. Where do you get off? It's idiotic…

MUNGO: (*Slight grin*) No, it's not … common sense, innit? More shots, Freddy…! What's wrong with hormones anyhow … should be proud of 'em. Part of Nature, innit? The mot wants to stay in the nest and sit on the eggs…

NAOMI: Eggs … eggs? What in Gawd's name are you talking about?

(MUNGO *drains both shots.*)

MUNGO: Did you want one as well…? Lookah, don't mind what those butch libbers do be tellin' ye. … Ye can't go against Nature… A good mot'll kill to save those eggs…

NAOMI: And the Lord and Master goes out hunting, I suppose…

MUNGO: Now ye have it. That's the way it has to be...

(*The music changes to a slow set, beginning with 'The Power of Love' by Jennifer Rush.*)

MUNGO: (*Hearing the song*) Tha's a fookin deadly track…

NAOMI: And have you been out hunting today, Mangow?

MUNGO: Yeah. Got a rapid little stash too. What d'ye think this is? (*He waves the joint in her face.*) Good shit. Try it.

NAOMI: No thanks…

MUNGO: Go on, it's good for you … makes the booze slide down … fookin' magic… (*He puts the joint near her lips.*)

NAOMI: I've never … done this before … (*She takes a couple of drags.*)

MUNGOW: You're born to it, Nomio. Get it right down into those sexy lungs.

NAOMI: (*Smiling*) It sort of grows on you…

MUNGO: Yeah it does grow on you. They don't call it 'weed' for nuttin'…

(*They dance in slow motion, about two feet between them.*)

NAOMI: It's good shit, Man…

MUNGO: Letting go a bit now, Nomio? Feel the effect? Hormones settling down … good … I like the lyrics on this one … they fry me

brains... This retro stuff is deadly…
(*They dance as the song builds up to the climactic chorus at which point* MUNGO *joins in.*)
'Cos I am your lady and you are my man …
whenever you reach for me I'll do all that I can
… whenever you reach for me I'LL DO ALL
THAT I C-A-AN' … for my MA-A-N …
Gerrit? What a set o' pipes on that broad.
That's a real woman for ye. None o' that libber shite…

NAOMI: (*Floating*) Sexist pig…

MUNGO: You got that right … I'm too sexy for me
shirt … (*Opens his shirt.*) Too sexy for me …
jocks … (*Gives a pelvic thrust.*) Jaysis, a guy'll
soon need permission in writin' for a bonk…
But sure that'd take all the good out of it …
should be spon … spontan … off the cuff, like
… somethin' like this, knowarIme-an?
(*He grabs her and shouts over his shoulder at the DJ.*)
Keep it goin', Jimmy. Tha' Whitney Houston is
brill…!
(*The volume increases as if 'Jimmy' is responding to the request, then drops down again after a few beats.*)

NAOMI: (*Tries to push him away but gives in*) You
like this, Mangow?

MUNGO: Rapid … can't beat a good lurch …
how're you doin'?

NAOMI: (*Flustered*) It's hot…

MUNGO: Name o' the game, Nomio.

(*He begins to nuzzle her face.*)
I'd like to … cover your body in … Flora margarine…

NAOMI: (*Hoarsely*) Kerrygold butter, nicer … scrambled egg if you like…

MUNGO: (*Huskily*) Eggs … yeah... Tie you up too … you'd like tha' … I can tell…

NAOMI: Mmmmnnnn … maybe … mmmmmmn…

MUNGO: And then a ninety-nine…

NAOMI: A *ninety*–nine…? That's an ice-cream…

MUNGO: Oh … yeah, slather on some strawberry ripple an all … along with the margarine. Fifty Shades o' Grey, like … I have a ball o' hairy twine too … an' a rubber-backed ping-pong bat … for a bit of spankin' like…

NAOMI: Sounds gooooood … mnnnnn ……

MUNGO: An a roll o' gaffer tape ……

NAOMI: Mnnnn … that's heavy, Mangow … gaffer tape … mnnnnnnnnnnn… You had me at 'hairy twine'…
(NAOMI'S *cell phone sounds with a classical-music ring tone. She hesitates. The music is halted while she answers the phone.*)
What? You can't cope…? Out of control…? Oh God… Right. OK, I said OK…
(*The 'Power of Love' music is restored.*)

MUNGO: (*Still floating*) What's happening?

NAOMI: (*Ordinary accent*) The baby-sitter can't cope with Emma and Jonathan. We'll have to go…

MUNGO: (*DORT accent*) Ow my Gawd. Some night out this proved to be. Just when it was

my turn to play the heavy. What an absolute
fiascow…

NAOMI: Well, that's turned me right off.

(*She picks up her bag.*)

MUNGO: Me too … my Gawd, after all the work I
put in … it's sow owful…

NAOMI: I hope we can get a taxi to Foxrock…
Remember, it's my turn to play the slag next
time…

(*They go towards the exit.*)

MUNGO: Of course, Dear. Fair's fair…

(*The 'Power of Love' music fades out.*)

Lights down.

END

SOCIAL CONSTRUCTS

NOTES FOR ACTORS

CECELIA and BELINDA are both attractive gay women living together. There are some unresolved issues between them. JACK is a bisexual man but with a preference for gay relationships. It is St. Patrick's Day.

Both women are talking in their apartment.

CECELIA: (*Tentatively*) Happy St. Patrick's Day to you, Belinda…

BELINDA: What's so happy about it, Cecelia…? St. Patrick was a homophobe, like most Christians.

CECELIA: Very true … but at least they're letting the LGBTI march in the parade this year… I have the shamrock here … will we march?

BELINDA: I'd love to support the LGBTI… I was going to march in the parade … I was looking forward to it … but not now… Lookit, I can't believe what you told me last night…

CECELIA: It wasn't easy for me to tell you, Belinda.

BELINDA: Well, it certainly wasn't easy for me to hear it. I'm still in a state of shock, Cecelia. I can't cope very well with change.

CECELIA: I suppose…

BELINDA: There's no supposing about it. I am deeply traumatised … I mean we were part of LGBTI for years … We were treated as criminals by the straight establishment … Church and State … and we fought and fought the powers that be… And eventually we won … we got a result.

CECELIA: Yes we did. It was a great result.

BELINDA: A terrific change … marriage equality under the law…

CECELIA: No doubt about it … a major breakthrough … a constitutional amendment, no less… It made international headlines.

Ireland has come of age.

BELINDA: And because of that breakthrough we were able to get married … you and me…

CECELIA: Yes we were … I remember the night I proposed.

BELINDA: So do I … in that club with Panti Bliss. It was wonderful. You went down on one knee…

CECELIA: And you nearly knocked me over when you threw your arms around me…

BELINDA: Well the ring was stunning … three carats … a lovely stone … yes … yes … that was then… Now you come along with this shocking news, Cecelia…

CECELIA: But it's not for the reasons you think… Anyway, it's not you … it's…

BELINDA: Me?

CECELIA: No. Me.

BELINDA: You?

CECELIA: Yes, me.

BELINDA: But why … why? Tell me why?

CECELIA: I don't know … I think I've always felt an urge, Belinda…

BELINDA: An urge…? What … a sort of niggle…?

CECELIA: Noooo … more an urge … a feeling I'm in the wrong body…

BELINDA: In the wrong body?

CECELIA: Yes … it never felt right… And the feeling gets stronger every day … at first I was just sort of … gender-fluid … but now the feeling is very strong ……

BELINDA: What kind of feeling exactly … apart

from the gender-fluidity…?

CECELIA: Well, for a long time I was gender non-conforming, then I became pangender… Now I'm non-binary…

BELINDA: Non-binary?

CECELIA: But then, as you know, I became a female … and I was cis-gender for a while… But now, I'm unhappy again…

BELINDA: Can you describe … how you feel?

CECILIA: Just … you know … wrong … I don't belong in a woman's body… It's hard to explain … top-heavy … I can't breathe … and I can't have … have…

BELINDA: Kids? No, of course not… But you must have known that before you transgendered…?

CECELIA: I didn't really focus on that. Not at the time … I thought … well, maybe I didn't think…

BELINDA: So now you want to become a man again…?

CECELIA: Now you have it… The whole hog … Female to Male … FTM… But of course I'm still in love with you, Belinda…

BELINDA: You are? I see… When you say you want to become a man, do you mean … in every way?

CECELIA: How do you mean, Belinda?

BELINDA: Well, with testosterone … all the appendages and stuff…

CECELIA: Oh yes … the lot… I know I'll probably have to go to Morocco to have the operation … they do very good work over there. … superb workmanship…

BELINDA: I don't want to hear about that… Why didn't you tell me all this *before* we got married?

CECELIA: I wasn't so sure then … gender-fluidity hadn't set in…

BELINDA: But you're sure now… So *I've* driven you to this…?

CECELIA: No, you haven't … it's just one of those things… Remember, the 'T' in LGBTI stands for Transgender … I may be transitioning, but I'll always be in love with you, Belinda.

BELINDA: How do you know how you'll feel after the operation?

CECELIA: Because we're *soul*mates, Belinda. It's not just physical…

BELINDA: I don't know, Cecelia … I just don't know… Suppose the operation makes you straight…?

CECILIA: It won't … but even if it did, would it make any difference? I'd still be the same person…

BELINDA: But you could be a hetero … they're such boring, stick-in-the-mud idiots.…

CECILIA: I know that. But I promise you I won't become a hetero. I've too much respect for myself.

BELINDA: Wait a sec… You'll be a man. But if you're gay you won't want me… If you were straight that wouldn't work either…

CECILIA: Don't worry, Belinda … it's not going to happen like that.

BELINDA: If you were still gay I'd have to become a man too… But I don't want to do that … oh the thought of it … oeeuff.

CECELIA: You're worrying too much … and over-analysing it… It'll be fine … wait and see…
(*They embrace.*)

BELINDA: Oh, I don't want you to go…

CECELIA: I have to … this body is killing me…
(*Lights down*)
(*Screen projection reads: "Cecilia travels to Morocco. The operation is successful. S/he waits until the scars have healed and then returns."*)

BELINDA: (*On phone*) I can't wait to see you, Cecilia … oh you're in a taxi already…? Yes, I'm looking forward to it … OK, see you soon … bye … bye…
(*Belinda tidies the apartment, and hides away a pair of men's shoes and a shirt.*)
I'm so confused … I don't really know how to handle this … Jack! Jack!
(JACK *enters.*)

BELINDA: Jack, she's on her way. You'd better keep out of sight when she arrives … 'He', I mean…

JACK: But you'll have to tell her about me sooner or later… I know she kept you in the dark for a long time about her gender reassignment … but you'll have to tell her you're bisexual – 'B' as in LG*B*TI. She's L and T. You're L and B…

BELINDA: Don't pressure me, Jack. I'll tell her in my own good time.

JACK: Well, suppose she wants to continue a lesbian relationship with you…? I mean you're still married.

BELINDA: How can she want that? She's a bloke now.

JACK: Suppose she, or he, wants a straight relationship with you? Where does that leave me?

BELINDA: Oh come on, Lover … is it likely that I'm going to prefer her / him to you…?

JACK: Well, you tell me?

BELINDA: Don't worry.

(*A bell sounds.*)

JACK: UH-Oh … the moment of truth.

BELINDA: Quick! Go into the bedroom … take that stuff with you…

(JACK *exits. Belinda admits* CECIL, *who has her / her hair tucked up under a baseball cap and is wearing jeans and a leather jacket. They embrace.* CECIL *does a twirl.*)

CECIL (*Deep voice*) Ta-Da! Well, what do you think?

BELINDA: You look great, Cecilia…

CECIL: It's Cecil now … but thanks…

BELINDA: Are you happy now … content?

CECIL: Oh yes. I did the right thing… My new body fits me like a glove … there are so many advantages to being a man…

BELINDA: Like what?

CECIL: Well, when I'm talking I get to the point much sooner … and, I can park a car now…

BELINDA: Hmmmmm! Anything else?

CECIL: I can reverse a car too … and read a map … and pee up against a wall… It's amazing … but here's the extraordinary thing…

BELINDA: What?

CECIL: I can't wash dishes anymore … they just fall out of my hands … and as for hoovering … forget about it…

BELINDA: I see … and … everything … is working all right?

CECIL: The new bits? Yes. Perfect working order… So how do we stand … marriage-wise…?

BELINDA: But you're not a lesbian anymore…

CECIL: Well, I'm the same person … with the same feelings…

BELINDA: But we're not a gay couple anymore … we'd be so ordinary and straight… I mean why go for mashed potato when you can have *pâté de foie gras*…? Straight people are just so damn boring … and colourless… You often said so yourself… I have to confess something Cecil…

CECIL: What?

BELINDA: I've been seeing someone else while you were away in Morocco … I had to … sort of … hedge my bets…

CECIL: You what…? I can't believe my ears … you're a transphobe…

BELINDA: I'm not a transphobe … but I have a man now … a real one … I mean a natural one… Sorry, it's all a bit confusing…

CECIL: But you're gay…

BELINDA: Actually, I swing both ways … I'm Bi

… give me a 'B'…

CECIL: OMG … But wait now … that means you
and I could get it on… You committed
adultery, but I could forgive you…

BELINDA: Well … yes we could get together
again… It's just that … well … Jack is more of
a man than you are … Jack!
(JACK *enters*.)

BELINDA: Sorry, Cecil … You're not in his league
… I'm sure you can see that…

CECIL: Oh, I don't know about that. What do you
say, Jack?

JACK: Well, you know me. I'm Bi too … but I
prefer gay relationships… Hetero ones are such
a pain … give me a 'G'…

BELINDA: What the hell's going on here?

CECIL: Jack and I go back a long way, Belinda. It's
because of him I got the gender
reassignment… Right, Jack?

BELINDA: You became a bloke to be with Jack…?
You're still gay but *male* gay? I don't believe
this…!

CECIL: We're also metrosexuals … at least for now.

JACK: Let's go, Cecil… Goodbye Belinda. It was
good while it lasted.
(*They link arms and exit*.)

BELINDA: Go on … feck off the lot of you … I
give up. You needn't come back to me looking
for my eggs… It's all too complicated for me.
I'm going to become a 'B' as in Bachelor. And
'C' as in celibate … or maybe … maybe I
could grasp the nettle and become …

straight... I've nothing left to lose.

(*She picks up the clump of withered shamrock.*)

BELINDA: Maybe I could follow in St Patrick's steps... Oh, no ... not possible ... no women priests allowed... Too bad ... I'd have to go to Morocco first ......

(*She crumples the shamrock.*)

Lights down.

END

PEER REVIEW

Daniel Maclise (1806-1870)
An Interview between Charles I and Oliver Cromwell, 1836
Oil on canvas, 184 x 235 cm
National Gallery of Ireland Collection
Photo © National Gallery of Ireland

NOTES FOR ACTORS

CÁITLÍN NÍ UALLACHÁIN is a youngish red-haired woman in period gown. Emotional. Used to hardship. Irish accent. JOHN BULL is a man with large belly, period costume, including red coat and riding boots. Phlegmatic and droll. Used to getting his own way. English accent.

JOHN *is on stage, studying a laptop and making occasional notes on a clipboard. The stage has a table and two chairs. It is actually a platform from which the actors can look down on Hell from every side. Railings would be useful though not essential.*

JOHN: Hmmmnnn… Maybe we need to turn up the heat in section seven … I'll keep an eye on it… Oh, damn, I have an apprentice arriving today … Kathleen … Kate something-or-other. A Colleen, I believe…

(JOHN *peers over one side of the stage, then goes to the screen and talks into a mic.*)

You … yes, you… Go back to Section five… Do it now … if not, you'll find yourself in the hottest pit… Go back if you know what's good for you…! (*To Himself*) There's always one who tries it on.

(*A knock on the door.* JOHN *looks over.* CÁIT *enters.*)

Ah Miss … Miss … Ni … Miss … Ni Huckel … Ni Huluk … Ni Hooll-a-chain..

CÁIT: Ní Uallacháin … Cáitlín Ní Uallacháin … I'm surprised you don't remember me, John … Anyway that's all blood under the bridge… You may call me Caitlin.

JOHN: I'm John … John Bull … well … you know… So, Kate it is… One is glad to meet you … For some reason, I was expecting someone older…

CÁIT: I used to be older, but after Independence I

was reborn.

JOHN: I see … no, I don't really, Kate…

CÁIT: Caitlin … I see you have a good view of Hell from this platform, John … all the souls paying the price for their earthly sins.

JOHN: Oh yes … Kathleen… We have the full 360-degree view here … And this is the latest computer with Google-Hellfire software… So Kathleen, you've been sent to me for some mentoring… One is happy to do it of course…

CÁIT: Mentoring … by you? Oh no … *one* is wrong about that… I've been given a roving brief to check on all administrators in the hell division. It's a sort of peer review. I've decided to start with you.

JOHN: (*Not really listening*) May I say you have a lovely brogue, Kathleen.

CÁIT: Let's keep this professional, John. I'm on secondment from Heaven to do this work. Part of my brief is to ensure that there have not been any miscarriages of justice … that the souls in eternal fire deserve to be there. So, yes, it is a peer review.

JOHN: Of course, one was a peer in a former life. A Knight actually … *Sir* John Bull.

CÁIT: Your title here is 'Administrator, Grade One', nothing else. And you got to Grade One on the basis of seniority.

JOHN: A peer review is hardly necessary. One doubts if the Almighty would have made any mistakes in sentencing these lost souls.

CÁIT: No one is disputing that. But there might

have been some ... ah ... slippage ... further down the chain of command. Besides, it's useful to double-check these things ... especially when dealing with eternity... Now I think I'll make a start. If you could show me the Irish section...

(*She and* JOHN *go to the laptop, study it for a while. Then they move to one side of the stage and look over the 'rail'.*)

I see ... Uh-hu ... uh-hu ... mmnnnn ... I see ... aha ... aha ... looks about right.

JOHN: Yes, everything is in order. You can see that the fieriest pit is reserved for Irish builders ... bankers ... junior ministers... At the back you have your property speculators ... and a smattering of what you called Blueshirts.

CÁIT: Mnnn ... mnnn ... Yes I can see that... There are also tax-dodgers ... phony socialists ... and ... traffic wardens in there... Fair enough... And that section to the left ... the one with huge flames and brimstone...? Who's in there? They must be real bad-asses...

JOHN: Clampers, I believe.

CÁIT: Clampers ... well that makes sense... And I think I can make out some lawyers as well ... I wouldn't argue with that...

JOHN: No surprises there, Kate. All cads and scoundrels.

CÁIT: (*Peering*) Ummmmnn ... but wait a minute ... hold on... Just behind that big mountain of sulphur and steam ... over where the lava is flowing ... who are those people...?

JOHN: People behind the … what people…?

CÁIT: Those … over there … oh my God … I know them … I know them very well … I can't believe…

JOHN: (*Uneasily*) Who…? What…?

CÁIT: They're Irish patriots…! What are they doing in there with all the bottom-feeders…?

JOHN: To whom do you refer…?

CÁIT: Are you blind? Those Irish patriots … there … suffering the torments of the damned … I can't believe it … Robert Emmet … Wolfe Tone … Parnell … Roger Casement … Michael Collins, even Daniel O'Connell…

JOHN: Well, they were rebels against the Crown … terrorists, one might say…

CÁIT: Terrorists? Terrorists? They were patriots, martyrs. They fought to free the motherland … me. They fought and suffered to free *me*, Caitlin Ni hUallachain!

JOHN: Well, they're paying the price now. Sorry about that, old girl.

CÁIT: Are you mad? Have you lost it completely?

JOHN: They wanted to die for their country, for *you*, and *you* call *me* mad?

CÁIT: An excess of love, Yeats called it. You wouldn't understand. You never did. Oh God, there's Patrick Pearse … beside a clamper… Such an indignity … the poor man… This is wrong, terribly wrong…

JOHN: They acted against the Crown, Kate. They could have destabilised the Empire… My God it doesn't bear thinking about.

CÁIT: Empires are vile... All that kept *us* going under the yoke of empire was the belief that things would be better in the next life. God would make it up to us in the Hereafter. That was all we had ... and now this... It's outrageous...

JOHN: Don't you think that's a little naïve, Kate?

CÁIT: Don't patronise me ... and it's Caitlin...

JOHN: I believe that modern historians take a different view of the Crown nowadays...

CÁIT: Oh, I've heard those historical revisionists too ... all UCD layabouts ... most of them should be in there with the clampers.

JOHN: Well, that's how it is, Kathleen. These sentences were decided at a very high level, way above your pay grade.

CÁIT: Well, it's wrong ... all wrong ... it's perverse... Maybe I'll get another perspective on it by looking at the English compound.
(JOHN *escorts her to the other side where they look over the 'rail' etc.*)

JOHN: All ship-shape and Bristol fashion as you can see. Even in Hell the English are well behaved. Good show, chaps ... Not like you Irish ... ahem... See over there ... we have English clampers in the brimstone section as well. So the penalties are the same.
(CÁIT *walks up and down.*)

CÁIT: Yes, that seems all right ... proportionate sentencing ... mnnn...

JOHN: You can see we have a special compound for investment bankers ... City of London and all that… And, of course, some of the Brexit lunatics…

CÁIT: Hmmmmnnn … that makes sense … I suppose… Wait now … hold on a wee second…

JOHN: (*Irritably*) Oeuffff … what now?

CÁIT: Do you know what I see?

JOHN: (*Wearily*) No. But I'm sure you're going to tell me.

CÁIT: Yes I am. I see absences.

JOHN: You see absences? As in, things that aren't there? Are you feeling all right, old girl?

CÁIT: Tell me this … where is Cromwell…? Where is Henry the Eighth…? Where is King William of Orange…? Where is General Maxwell…? Where are the Black and Tans…? Where is *Trevelyan*…?!

JOHN: They're … aam … not there. It would appear that they are absent…

CÁIT: Why aren't they there? My God, when I think of the Famine, the Penal Laws, Plantations… Why are those responsible not paying the price?

JOHN: They were found innocent by due process.

CÁIT: I can't believe my ears…! Are you saying they all went to heaven?

JOHN: Some spent a little time in Purgatory … a slap on the wrist so to speak.

CÁIT: Cromwell got a slap on the wrist? I don't believe this! Punish the innocent and reward the guilty. This is a travesty!!

JOHN: Come on Kate. What's done is done… One

has to accept the inevitable.

CÁIT: Don't call me Kate…! What's done can be undone!

JOHN: Due process, Kathleen … impeccable procedures were followed.

CÁIT: I'm going to have to report this in the strongest possible terms. I will be recommending that each case be thoroughly reviewed.

JOHN: But that would create an appalling vista. One must maintain confidence in the judicial system at all costs. Think of the colonies … the poor people who look up to us…

CÁIT: That's it, isn't it? Don't question imperial decisions…! What about 'justice though the heavens fall'…? Oh, I'm going to write a very strongly worded report on this. Count on it.

JOHN: I'll have to vet it before you send it on.

CÁIT: No. I'm going over your head.

JOHN: You can't … the chain of command… Look, Kathleen, try to be more stoical … accept the inevitable… That's the trouble with you Irish … always questioning your betters.

CÁIT: Betters? Betters? That's it! Enough! I'm going straight to God about this.

JOHN: It won't do you any good, old girl.

CÁIT: Oh? And why is that?

JOHN: Didn't you know…? God favours the big battalions. Might is right … always has been. The meek may inherit the earth but they get bugger all of the Hereafter.

CÁIT: We're dealing with Divine justice here … not

what passes for British justice. I can fix this. Don't you worry.

JOHN: No, you can't.

CÁIT: *One* seems very sure of *one*self…!

JOHN: Yes. Because one knows things…

CÁIT: Such as?

JOHN: Can you handle the truth, Kathleen?

CÁIT: Try me.

JOHN: Well, it turns out … that God is English…

CÁIT: Don't be ridiculous!

JOHN: Why would one lie? He's from Essex. He's also Protestant … Church of England … So you see, Kathleen, you can't win. The Mainland always dominated your small island. The cards are stacked and there's not a damn thing you can do. Remember the slogan: *'To Hell or to Connaught'*? It's a pity more of your rebels didn't go to Connaught … they wouldn't have ended up here. Sorry, old girl, but that's how it is.

CÁIT: OK, Mr. appalling vista … OK, old boy … Sean Tarbh … let me explain something … I've been testing you…

JOHN: You testing me…? That's rich … I think you may be losing your mind, Kate.

CÁIT: Not I … John … do you know what this is? (*She shows him a card.*)

JOHN: (*Shocked*) That doesn't … belong … to … you…!

CÁIT: Oh but it does.

JOHN: It couldn't…

CÁIT: Oh yes, it could and does… You can verify if

you like … go ahead, make my day.
(*She hands it to him and he slots it into the laptop. He resiles in shock.*)

JOHN: I'm … I'm … so sorry, Ms Ni hUallachain … I didn't know…

CÁIT: Well, you do now.

JOHN: (*Breathless*) May one ask when … you were … elevated…?

CÁIT: I was elevated to Archangel quite recently, John … shortly before I took on this assignment.

JOHN: I should have been more … cooperative with you … I'm sorry…

CÁIT: I want all the sentences reviewed. I believe you lied at the trials. Do you know the punishment for celestial perjury? You will have to purge your contempt … more than ten thousand years of cleansing fire, I would think. You will have to dismantle the Empire piece by piece. There will also be a charge of defamation. You said God is English. That is defamatory. Everyone knows He's from Munster.

JOHN: (*Desperately*) But … but … this is entrapment … a sting … It won't stand up…

CÁIT: Really John. Really? Is that the best you can do?

JOHN: I'm sorry, I don't mean that… It's all such a shock … I'm sure we can work something out, old girl … sorry … Your Eminence … Please don't bring me to trial… The sentences will be changed … colonies freed … but don't tell on me…

CÁIT: I'm not vindictive. We'll see…

(*He falls to his knees, and begins to weep. He shuffles towards her on his knees.*)

JOHN: Thank you! Oh thank you … I was only a peer … you are peerless … I was under pressure to be tough … live up to my name, John Bull … lot of peer pressure … I'm sure you understand … sorry for everything … past and present … if one could change history … but one can't … can't…

CÁIT: Oh get up. I can't stand to see a grown man cry… Man up … grow a pair…

JOHN: (*Kisses her feet and struggles to stand.*) I will … I'll try … whatever you say, Your Angelic Highness…

Lights down.

END

SEXUAL MINDFULNESS

NOTES FOR ACTORS

ROB, an ageing farmer, has invited MATTY, who is younger though more a man of the world, to his cottage for some important advice. ROB is reluctant to reveal any information about himself. As a Louth man he doesn't pronounce his 'Ts'. MATTY, a blow-in from Cork, isn't as knowledgeable as he thinks he is.

The two farmers are sitting in front of the fire in an old-fashioned kitchen.

ROB: Ye'll have some jelly 'n custard, Mahhi?

MATTY: I won't say no, Rob. Since ye asked me here this evening.

(ROB *spoons it out into saucers from an old saucepan.*)

Nice! The childer go mad for this, Rob.

ROB: I wouldn't know about tha.

MATTY: Oh they lash it down.

ROB: I knew ye had a swee tooh, Mahhi.

MATTY: And yerself, I'd say.

ROB: Ah no. The swee tooh fell out … along wi the pipe tooh.

MATTY: Oh yeah, ye don't puff the pipe anymore. I noticed that.

ROB: Sure ye can't. Not when the pipe tooh falls out on ye. Ye've nohing then to hold the shank wi. The gums wouldn't do the job ah all. Noh withou the tooh.

MATTY: I can see that. Still, you're better off not smoking.

ROB: They say ye're behher off awrigh withou the nicohine … Buh I still have the cough. Can't shake ih off ah all.

MATTY: Why did ye ask me here, Rob?

ROB: Ye'r a greah man for the knowledge. None behher, Mahhi … Buh we'll geh to tha by n' by. The nigh is young.

MATTY: Not too young I hope.

(*They fall silent for a while eating the jelly and custard.*)

MATTY: Did ye have the heifer in the fair on Tuesday?

ROB: Wha heifer?

MATTY: The little black 'n white one above in the top field.

ROB: *My* top field?

MATTY: (*Irritable*) No the top field in … in … Ethiopia … or maybe the one in the Tibetan Plateau.

ROB: I've no field in Ehiopia … or the Tibehan Plaho…

MATTY: Oh do ye not? It must be the field near the road to Termonfeckin so… Tell me, did the little heifer make a good price at the fair?

ROB: Eh … what fair is tha, Mahhi?

MATTY: Forget I asked, Rob! (*Aside*) Cute hoor to the end.

ROB: What did ye say, Mahhi?

MATTY: Nothing at all…

ROB: Will ye have a lihhle more jelly 'n custard?

MATTY: Aye, I will thanks. I used to love it as a chisler in Cork. Before I dandered up to this neck o' the woods.

(ROB *exits to get more jelly.* MATTY *flicks through a nearby pile of newspapers and magazines.*)

ROB (*Dishes out*) There ye are now, another plahher o' the good stuff, Mahhi.

(MATTY *fishes out a blob of white oatmeal.*)

MATTY: What's this?

ROB: Could be a bih a' stirabout left in the poh, Mahhi.

MATTY: (*Impatient*) Hmmmnn…! So did ye want to ask me somethin', Rob?

ROB: I suppose I did.

MATTY: What?

ROB: Ah, ye know…

MATTY: No, I don't know. How would I know unless ye tell me? It's called giving information.

ROB: I thou ye'd guess.

MATTY: How would I guess? Is it about a third world war with nuclear bombs? Or maybe it's a volcanic eruption over in Drumsna?

ROB: Ah no. Nohing like tha.

MATTY: So what is it?

ROB: (*Slowly*) Well, ye know I've lived on me own for a good while now…

MATTY: Forty years I'd say.

ROB: There or thereabouh … an no chick or child.

MATTY: A confirmed bachelor … tis not so unusual around here.

ROB: (*Slowly*) Well … amn't I after meehing somewan…

MATTY: Someone? Who?

ROB: Ah, ye know like…

MATTY: Hmmmmnnn. The AI man? A fire-eater maybe? An alien from Jupiter?

ROB: No. A … woman.

MATTY: A woman?
(ROB *nods.*)

MATTY: That's a bit of a surprise.

ROB: I suppose ih is, Mahhi.

MATTY: And what d'ye want to know?

ROB: Ih's all a bih new to me. There's a lohha things to find ouh.

MATTY: Before I give you the benefit of me advice I want you to tell me something.

ROB: Wha?

MATTY: How much did ye get for the little heifer?

ROB: Wha heifer…?

MATTY: (*Rising*) I'm goin … I've more important things to be doin'…

ROB: (*Squeaking*) Three hunerd euros!

MATTY: Hmmmnnn … ye were robbed…! What d'ye want to know? How to get her to go out?

ROB: The heifer?

MATTY: The woman! This new woman of yours. Who is she anyway?

ROB: Wha d'ye mean?

MATTI: Who is she? Elizabeth Taylor, Marilyn Monroe, Mary Robinson, Biddy in Glenroe…?

ROB: None o' them. She's behher than them, a loh behher…

MATTI: (*Gives up*) So, you want to know how to ask her out? Is that it?

ROB: No, sure we've been ouh already…

MATTY: For walks like?

ROB: No. More than tha'. We went to Ardee and Termonfeckin. We had fish suppers … bahhered cod … bahhered sausages … the loh.

MATTY: That's a fright. Ye're a big spender, Rob.

ROB: I'm a bih slow to start … the price o' things now'd friken ya … buh when I geh goin I'm arigh…

MATTY: Sure your suckin diesel now with your fish suppers an' battered sausages. So you want to know what comes next?

ROB: Kind of…

MATTY: (*Without much hope*) Do I know the lady? Is she from around here?

ROB: (*Lying*) No. No, ye wouldn't know her, noh ah all.

MATTY: (*Sighs*) Well, what age is she … roughly?

ROB: Ah sure how would I know tha … the ladies do be slow to tell ya things like tha…

MATTY: They're not the only ones … *you're* no spring chicken.

ROB: She don't mind tha. Nah wan bih … sure she's after acceptin' ……

MATTY: Accepting what?

ROB: I asked for her hand, like…

MATTY: Her hand? D'ye not want the rest of her?

ROB: I do so … after we get wed…

MATTY: What d'ye want my advice for. The hard part is over. You're not a bad little operator there, Rob, behind the scenes.

ROB: Well, I was readin' some magazines … an it's a bih of a puzzle…

MATTY: What is?

(ROB *drops a piece of jelly, scoops it up from the floor with a spoon and puts it back in his saucer.*)

ROB: Like whah ye're supposed to do after the marriage…

MATTY: Ye must have a fair idea after lookin' at

cattle an' sheep for sixty years.

ROB: Yeah, buh I think it'd be different wih wimmin.

MATTY: Are ye in good workin order?

ROB: Yah. Good enough. Could be fihher tho.

MATTY: I mean down below.

ROB: Oh, down below…? Where d'ye mane?

MATTY: You know damn well. Does it work?

ROB: How would I know…? I'm a bachelor ……

MATTY: (*Irritable*) Yer not St Francis of Assisi… Does the feckin' thing work? Does it obey orders?

ROB: Most o' the time anaways … as far as I can tell…

MATTY: As far as ya can tell! Well, ye can get stuff nowadays. Vigara … It's not a problem anymore.

ROB: It's kinda more than tha, Mahhi.

MATTY: What now?

ROB: It says in the magazines tha the wimmin expect more things nowadays…

MATTY: What class o' things?

ROB: Strange doings, Mahhi …' twould friken ye a bih…

MATTY: What things? Holidays in hotels, central heating, going to the cinema…?

ROB: No … (*Beat*) … things in the bed … different ways o' doing things…

MATTY: Look Rob. Ye can forget about all that Hollywood stuff. I mean did ye ever see a bull smackin' a cow's arse? Or a ram pissin all over a ewe? No, you did not. Because them things

239

are not natural. Ye can't have a better guide than nature. D'ye follow me?

ROB: Buh … I mane … there are different ways o' getting' tangled up, like … ways ya wouldn't think a … a leg here, an arm there … ye know wha I mane…

MATTY: And what about your religion? Them funny things are sins. Yes, even in marriage. The Pope himself said so in a Papal Bull… And think o' your poor sainted mother looking down on ye from Heaven … having to look at them knots and tangles … and her firstborn son's backside… She'd be disgusted… Take my advice. Cut out the fancy stuff. That's not for the likes of us. 'Tis only for film stars and them actors up in Dublin…

ROB: 'Tisn't really the fancy stuff, Mahhi … (*Beat*) … 'Tis somethin' called the … 'The big O'. 'Tis in all the magazines.

MATTY: (*Slightly relieved*) Oh!

ROB: Yah, 'O'. The big O. I mane wha is ih? Wha is ih in the world o' Gawd?

MATTY: Well, let me put it like this. Ye know the kind of farmin' we do…?

ROB: Yah. A bih o this, a bih o tha.

MATTY: Then there's the smart lads that do Organic farming. Are ye with me?

ROB: The Organic stuff is supposed to be behher.

MATTY: Yah, it's supposed to be. D'ye get me now? Organic, like. Better … d'ye see?

ROB: No, Mahhi … noh ah all… Wha's the big O thing tha wimmin want?

MATTY: (*Thoughtful*) Em … put it like this. You're playing a football match. There's only a minute to go. You need a point to win. You go on a solo run. Then you kick the ball. Yer heart is pounding. You watch the ball go up in the air. Will it go over the bar or not? The wind is strong. It looks like the ball is going wide. Then at the last second a gust o' wind blows it over the bar. Your team wins. How would you feel?

ROB: Jayz, I'd feel greah, Mahhi … mihie … I'd feel mihie.

MATTY: Well, that's how the women like to feel at the end…

ROB: Oh yeah, yeah… Buh waih a minuh … wimmin don' play foohball, Mahhi.

MATTY: (*Irritable*) It's the ending … the ending … it's somethin' that happens to them at the end of the…

ROB: Ah the end o' wha, Mahhi?

MATTY :(*Loud*) At the full time whistle…! At the end of what ye'd be at in the bed…
(*Pause while* ROB *reflects. He screws up his face, purses his mouth etc.*)

MATTY: What's wrong with ye now? Amn't I after explainin'…?

ROB: I don righly know … I wus brough up to … I always though tha the fair sex only puh up wih ih to have babies, like…

MATTY: Oh yeah … Sugar an' spice an' all things nice… But that was all wrong. Women like it just as much as us … maybe more…

ROB: Ah now, Mahhi … Are ye sure abouh tha?

MATTY: O' course I'm sure… And by the way, down in Cork, the women do play football … and whenever they score a point or a goal, you should hear the roarin outta them. Sure, they're human beings like us.

ROB: You tell me so?

MATTY: I do. Look at it like this. Women suffer the pains of having childer. Why would they go through that if there was nothing in it for them. 'Course they enjoy a bit o' the other.
(*Another pause for reflection.* ROB *puts a sod on the fire and uses a pitchfork to stir the embers.*)
What now?

ROB: The big O thing happens to *them* … so there's nothing *I* have to do, like?

MATTY: Well, there is… How can I put this? Ye know how ye have to warm up before a match. Well, ye have to help the woman to warm up too. Only it takes longer. D'ye see?

ROB: Stretchin' an' doin' exercises?

MATTY: Well, a bit o' massage wouldn't go astray. But other things too. Compliments, encouragement, a bit o' humour, a bag o' sweets … Peppermint Lumps maybe or chewing-gum for the match. Buh nothing rushed or forced. No that wouldn't do at all. Everything should be nice and slow … aisy and natural.

ROB: Yeah. Buh tha's in the dressing room… Wha' abouh … I mean wha' abouh laher on in the bed…?

MATTY: Ye have to slow down there as well … take it aisy like … for five or six minutes anyways…

ROB: Five or six minutes? Jaze tha's a long time, Mahhi. How would ye do tha?

MATTY: Well, ye have to distract yerself. Think of somethin' else … some lads think of their Mammies.

ROB: I couldn't do tha, Mahhi. Ah God no. Noh tha. Noh the Mammy…

MATTY: Well then, think of the worst thing ye have to do on the farm.

ROB: Like … pullin a cow outta a drain in the lashin' rain?

MATTY: That might work. Anything else?

ROB: I could think o' the ould red sehher savagin' me sheep. Or a fox scahherring me chickens.

MATTY: They'd be good too.

ROB: Yah, I might geh five minutes ouhha them two or three things.

MATTY: Yah. And then she'll get the big O … the winnin' point o' the game … without any of that fancy stuff… And the job's oxo… So, are ye all right now?

ROB: I'm behher than I was, Mahhi… Buh wha exachly is the big O? Ya didn't say. Noh really.

MATTY: Ah 'tis something the wimmin know about. It's a kind of a secret thing. They wouldn't like us knowing it.

ROB: Why? It might puh 'em off, like? No big O if they knew we knew abou ih?

MATTY: Exactly, Rob … Now ye have it … tis private information … *you'd* understand that…
(MATTY *stands and stretches.*)
Well, me work here is done.

ROB: There's one odder thing, Mahhi.

MATTY: (*Sighs*) What's that?
(ROB *looks around and then whispers in his ear and shows him the magazine.*)

MATTY: (*Jumps aside*) Not a chance. I'm not tellin ya anything about that … it's too much … forget about that …'tis against the law.

ROB: But accordin' to the buke 'tis an imporhant mahher.

MATTY: For heathens maybe … you'll go straight to hell if you try that. I'll have nothing to do with explaining that to you. I'm feckin' off outta here.

ROB: Well, thanks anaway, Mahhi. Don't forget yer cap.

MATTY: G'night now. Take my advice. Bring them books out to the haggard and burn them.
Thanks for the jelly and custard. Oh, and good luck with the wedding.

ROB: Thanks, Mahhi. G'night.
(MATTY *exits.* ROB *looks at the magazine again, turning it sideways and upside down. He looks shocked at first but then begins to smile.*)
Mahhi is a bih seh in his ways… You'd see him of a Sunday, atin the feeh off the stahues…
(*He looks at the magazine, nods and grins.*)
This cavorshion is a bih complicahed all righ

... buh I think I can geh the hang of ih ... if I practise enough...
(*He turns the magazine this way and that.*)
Jaze, I'd need to limber up for tha ... I'd have to be rale fih to score tha last goal.
(*He continues to consult the magazine as the lights are dimmed.*)

Lights down.

END

AS YOU WERE

A Radio Play

NOTES FOR ACTORS

The main character, THOMAS, is a harmless, lonely man approaching middle age. The play revolves around discussions he has with two friends, MINNIE and HARRY, about the novel he is working on. They debate the plot and style of the novel, and advise him about whether or not it should be more literary or more commercial. There are disagreements and heated exchanges – and moments of interior monologue where Thomas recalls painful aspects of his youth.

It is clear that Thomas is deeply in love with Minnie, and rather jealous of Harry.

It gradually emerges that Thomas's 'friends' are products of his imagination – characters he would have in a book if he were writing one. Despite his mental state, he is happy in the company of his 'characters'. It is as if they are real friends. They pose little threat to him since they are products of his imagination. He has in a way created a stable environment for himself to live in, having been released from a mental hospital.

The 'characters' realise that if he doesn't write more commercially he might not be asked to do sequels, in which case they'll die. He is saddened by this and resolves to help them as best he can...

They are all happy with the decision arrived at, and they toast each other...

But the local shopkeeper, who keeps an eye on Thomas, suspects that he has gone off the rails again. She calls his psychiatrist...

The main question posed by the play is whether medical intervention might ruin the kind of benign environment Thomas has invented for himself, to make his life worthwhile.

A. Exterior. Night. Sound of bus coming to a stop on a wet street. Footsteps on pavement.

1. THOMAS: (INTERIOR MONOLOGUE) Nearly home … just one message to do … bread and ham, two slices … a loaf and two slices of ham… one loaf… Remember that.

(*Sound of shop bell tinkling.*)

B. Interior of shop. Sound of cash register. Mood music: Irish C& W.

1. WOMAN SHOP-OWNER: Damp old evening, Thomas.

2. THOMAS: (ABSENT-MINDEDLY) Wha-at? Oh .. yes .. yes it is ..damp … Mrs … em…

3. WOMAN SHOP-OWNER: The usual is it, Thomas? A loaf and two slices of ham?

4. THOMAS: That's it … yes please.

   (*Sounds of bacon slicer, rummaging, coins being placed on counter.*)

5. WOMAN SHOP-OWNER: There you are now. A nice pan-loaf and two lean slices of ham. And your change.

6. THOMAS: Thank you, Mrs … eh…

   (*Shop bell tinkles. Footsteps. Door opens and shuts.*)

7. WOMAN SHOP-OWNER: Poor old soul. Gold watch and no breakfast.

C. Interior of apartment block. Footsteps stop at a door.

Sounds of several locks being opened. Door opens and closes. Keys turn in locks. Sounds of bread being buttered. Then chewing sounds.

1. THOMAS: (INTERIOR MONOLOGUE) The cat must be out … I'll leave a bit of ham for him. I wonder if the others are inside?

   (*Sound of internal door opening*)

2. MINNIE: (THEATRICALLY, SEDUCTIVELY) I've been waiting for you, Thomas. You shouldn't keep a girl waiting.

3. THOMAS: (FLUENTLY) Hello, Minnie. How long have you been here?

4. MINNIE: (HUSKILY) Too long, lover. You look tired. Some music might help.

(*Sound of Enya-style romantic music*)

5. THOMAS: Would you like some of my sandwich Minnie? Ham only. I thought I had some cheese but I think the mouse got it.

6. MINNIE: I'll pass, Thomas dear. Come over here and sit by me… Oh, you're so tense. Let me ease these knotted muscles.

7. THOMAS: Mmmmmmm … mmmmmmm. That feels wonderful.

8. MINNIE: You deserve the best, Baby.

9. THOMAS: You're not trying to get around me, Minnie? Are you?

10. MINNIE: As if I would. You're always so suspicious and negative, Thomas. I'm doing this for you. For you, not for me.

11. THOMAS: Sorry, Minnie. It's just that I don't normally … I'm not that attractive to…

12. MINNIE: Women? How can you say that? You're a Doll. Boyish and manly at the same

time.

13. THOMAS: (INTERIOR MONOLOGUE) Is she overdoing it a bit? God, who cares? This massage is fabulous.

14. MINNIE: You question everything, Thomas. You should stop it and accept things at face value.

15. THOMAS: Minnie, you are a wonder. You can read me like a book... And I should stop being so negative. I should... (INTERIOR MONOLOGUE) Though it wasn't easy growing up. Not easy. Hard to forget...

D. FLASHBACK. Melange of harsh voices. Different tone to indicate FLASHBACK. Cacophonous music.

1. TEACHER'S VOICE: Believe it or not, Class, Thomas can't even memorise his Catechism. Put out your hand ... you dope...

(*Sound of three smacks followed by cries.*)

2. UNCLE'S VOICE: Your mother's been put in the Magdalene Laundry ... she's fallen ... a fallen ... woman.

3. EMPLOYER'S VOICE: I did your uncle a favour giving you this job ... and this is how you repay me ... get out of it...

4. ALL THREE VOICES: Dope ... repay me ... fallen ... need to be punished...

5. THOMAS: (INTERIOR MONOLOGUE) Noo, nooo ... try to forget...

E. Interior Thomas's flat

1. THOMAS: Oh, God...

2. MINNIE: Look, we all have bad memories. Put them out of your mind.

3. THOMAS: Well, at least we're OK now. All of us here. Together.

4 MINNIE: Are we OK?

5 THOMAS: What do you mean?

6. MINNIE: Well, for one thing, I'm not happy with the quarry. It's not suitable. Nothing romantic can happen in a quarry.

7. THOMAS: (INTERIOR MONOLOGUE) I knew there was something. Oh, Minnie, Minnie, Minnie…

(*Sound of a cigarette being lit.*)

8. THOMAS: Must you smoke?

9. MINNIE: Yes I must. Don't be such a tight ass.

10. THOMAS: It's my lungs I'm worried about.

11. MINNIE: And another thing … I'm not happy with Harry Haines.

12. THOMAS: Oh Harry is all right. Basically. His bark is worse than his bite. Besides, there's no one…

13. MINNIE: Sssssh. It's him … I know it's him.

(*Sound of door opening. Music changes to something more up-tempo.*)

14. MINNIE: Speak of the devil. (INTERIOR MONOLOGUE) God this is all I need. Harry Haines as I live and breathe.

15. HARRY: (BREEZILY) At your service, one and all. Thought I should put in an appearance.

16. MINNIE: Since you're here, let me ask you something.

17. HARRY: Shoot, Darlin'.

18. MINNIE: What do you think about the quarry?

19. HARRY: No skin off my teeth. If that's where the body part is, so be it.

20. MINNIE: And that's another thing … the damn body part. It's vulgar and melodramatic.

21. HARRY: Oh, I don't know about that. It'll add frisson to our date, Minnie.

22. THOMAS: (INTERIOR MONOLOGUE) I don't like this at all. What's happening? They should be in agreement…

23. MINNIE: You can forget about it, Harry.

24. HARRY: Look, we're lovers. That's what lovers do … have frisson.

25. THOMAS: (INTERIOR MONOLOGUE) Oh God, I've fallen for her. She's not my type. She's uppity and full of herself. But I'm jealous of Harry. I can't deny it.… Look at how her hair cascades over her forehead. She's a beautiful woman. I'm in big trouble. I never

thought this could happen to me again.

26. MINNIE: Thomas, I thought you cared
    something for me. Why do you put me in
    sordid situations? Have I offended you in some
    way?

27. THOMAS: No, absolutely not. … it's … it's my
    fault … some unresolved … issues … baggage
    from the past… Forget it … put it behind…
    Christ, here it comes…

*F. Flashback. Melange of voices. Different tone to
    indicate FLASHBACK. Cacophonous music.*

1. EMPLOYER'S VOICE: You're bloody useless.
   Pick up your cards on the way out…

2. UNCLE'S VOICE: (INTERRUPTING) She left
   you her prayer-book, Thomas. Nothing else.
   She's gone into an unmarked grave. You'll
   never know where…

3. TEACHER'S VOICE: (INTERRUPTING) Go up
   to the punishment room, boy, and strip off.
   Now! Run, you little bastard!

4. ALL THREE VOICES: Useless little shit…
   You're fired… Spawn of a fallen woman…

Nothing but trouble ever since you got here…
Go up to the punishment room, boy…
Take your punishment like a man… Stop
whimpering… Strip off … strip . …. you little
bastard … (VOICES FADE AWAY).

5. THOMAS: (INTERIOR MONOLOGUE, LONG
    AGONISING GROAN, PUNCTUATED BY:)
    Oh God, Oh God, Oh God…

G. Interior Thomas's Flat.

1. MINNIE: We need to sit down and talk this
    through. Calmly. I'm going to put the kettle on.

    (*Sounds of kettle being filled.*)

2. HARRY: Talking never hurt anyone … I've
    nothing to be afraid of…

3. MINNIE: Oh no? Are you sure about that?

4. THOMAS: The important point is that we're an
    ensemble. We're all in this together.

5. HARRY: (CLAPS HANDS SARCASTICALLY)
    Nice one, Thomas. Empathy. You engage with
    us. So everyone's happy. Very convenient. But
    you get your way, of course.

6. MINNIE: (WHEEDLING) You know, guys. The quarry and all that … it's a little downmarket, don't you think?

7. THOMAS: I don't think we should be snobbish about this … sorry Minnie…

8. HARRY: There's nothing wrong with action and romance. But then I'm not an intellectual. I don't listen to Bach fugues all day while meditating on the meaning of life. Or maybe I'm just not pretentious…

    (*Sounds of water boiling, tea being made, cups being distributed.*)

9. MINNIE: (ANGRILY) Are you suggesting that I…?

10. THOMAS: Easy on … easy. Actually, Harry, I think you are more reflective than you pretend.

11. HARRY: Look, I'm a straightforward sort of bloke. Nothing fancy or complicated. What you see is what you get. We're all cut from the same cloth, if you want my opinion.

12. MINNIE: Speak for yourself. You may not be a fully rounded person but please don't include me in that category. And Thomas, I'm

surprised at you of all people. I would appreciate it if you might stop pushing me into situations which are inappropriate. The quarry scene is not me.

13. THOMAS: Minnie, we all have to be reasonable… (INTERIOR MONOLOGUE) Much as I love her I can't really give in on this point… Wait now, is there something else on her mind? Something deeper? She seems to be more agitated than usual.

14. HARRY: Yes, reasonable. Well done, Thomas, you're beginning to stand up to her. It's never too late to grow a set of balls…

15. MINNIE: You lout! How dare you speak to Thomas like that, and use such language in front of me.

16. HARRY: Minnie, I know you, remember? I know you.

17. MINNIE: I haven't the faintest idea what you're talking about. I am simply trying to make a point about artistic integrity. Where that is concerned there is no question of compromise. There is a line I will not cross.

18. THOMAS: Minnie, we all have to compromise. Let's face it, we're trying to meet a public demand. Maybe the public is fickle or

superficial. But we can't dictate to them.

19. MINNIE: What of absolutes?

20. THOMAS: (SADLY) There aren't any.

21. MINNIE: I refuse to believe that. If that were true then life would not be worth living.

22. THOMAS: (INTERIOR MONOLOGUE) Oh Minnie, Minnie, you are a wonder. I'm crazy about you. And you defended me when Harry called me a coward.

   (*Sound of knocking on apartment door.*)

23. THOMAS: Oh my God, who's that?

   (*Sounds of chair scraping, several locks being undone, door being carefully opened.*)

H. Interior. Corridor outside Thomas's Flat.

1. WOMAN SHOP-OWNER: Thomas, I was out walking and...

2. THOMAS: Oh, Mrs ... em ... (INTERIOR MONOLOGUE) Christ, what does she want?

3. WOMAN SHOP-OWNER: Yes, and I found your cat…

(*Sound of cat meowing.*)

4. THOMAS: Mr Puddle … my cat … yes. I forgot about him. Sorry, Mr Puddle … come here…

5. WOMAN SHOP-OWNER: Cats need to be looked after, Thomas. This isn't the first time I found him wandering…

6. THOMAS: It won't happen again. Thanks for … bringing him back … (INTERIOR MONOLOGUE) Go, go, please go … you interfering old busybody…

7. WOMAN SHOP-OWNER: Have you got cat food in the fridge?

8. THOMAS: Oh yes … plenty…

9. WOMAN SHOP-OWNER: (SUSPICIOUSLY) Kitekat or Mogchunks?

10. THOMAS: Both.

11. WOMAN SHOP-OWNER: I don't stock those brands.

12. THOMAS: There are … other shops …

(INTERIOR MONOLOGUE) They eat mice, you know… Please go. Go now.

13. WOMAN SHOP-OWNER: Have you company this evening, Thomas? I thought I heard…

14. THOMAS: Oh yes … yes indeed. Actually, I'd better, you know … get back … to my guests… Thanks again … for Mr Puddle…

15. WOMAN SHOP-OWNER: Are you all right, Thomas…? Would you like me to call … anyone?

16. THOMAS: (ABRUPTLY) No … no thanks … I have to get back to … my guests now… (INTERIOR MONOLOGUE) Why don't you just mind your own business and feck off out of it…?

I. Interior Thomas's Flat.

(Sounds of door being closed, several locks being fastened.)

1. MINNIE: Ah, Mr. Puddle. I wondered where you'd got to.

2. THOMAS: He likes you, Minnie. He always

makes for your lap.

(*Sounds of purring.*)

3. MINNIE: I hope he's not moulting. This skirt's angora.

4. HARRY: Could we forget about Mr Piddle for a while?

5. THOMAS: Mr Puddle.

6. HARRY: Whatever… The fact is that Minnie is making life difficult for us all. She'll just have to accept reality, warts and all.

7. MINNIE: I've got an even better idea. Why not scrap Harry as well as the quarry scene? I could meet Justin instead. In an Art Gallery, say. Think of the chemistry, the meeting of minds. I'm amazed you never thought of it.

8. THOMAS: (INTERIOR MONOLOGUE) I have thought of it and it scares me to death. You could really fall for Justin. This is not going to happen.

9. HARRY: He's gay. It wouldn't lead anywhere.

10. MINNIE: Au contraire. He's a real man and I should know… Ow! Ow! The damn cat just

scratched me.

(*Loud Meows and sounds of a cat scampering away.*)

11. THOMAS: Your idea is a good one, Minnie, though a little contrived. The problem is that a meeting of minds is not good theatre. There's no conflict. Anyway, the public prefer a bit of rough, as the saying goes.

12. HARRY: Down and dirty pays the rent.

13. MINNIE: Thomas, Thomas, Thomas, you're so cautious… Take a chance. If you had real talent you could make my idea work. Suspend disbelief and all that.

14. THOMAS: (INTERIOR MONOLOGUE) What if she's right? If I've no talent then I'm done for. I might as well go back to the orphanage or some other institution.

15. MINNIE: Harry thinks he's Action Man or some predictable moron. Well I'm different. I often behave out of character…

16. HARRY: That's just hormones acting up.

17. MINNIE: It's what makes a woman interesting.

(The Enya-style mood music changes to 'Ode to Billy Joe', instrumental only.)

18. THOMAS: That may be true. But these more untypical traits have to be left out. One has to concentrate solely on the dominant characteristics.

19 HARRY: Before he gets the verbal trots, why can't you give a little, Minnie? Let him do the simple commercial stuff. The world needs that as well as the fancy stuff. We are needed … as we are… And you know something else? You're not really listening to Thomas…

20. MINNIE: Of course I am.

21. HARRY: (SERIOUSLY) I don't think so. What I hear him saying is … kind of worrying.

22. MINNIE: And what might that be, Dr. Freud?

23. HARRY: If we don't do the quarry scene, if you don't lower your high-falutin' standards, there may not be any sequels…

(Beat)

24. MINNIE: (AGHAST) My God … is that what … you're saying, Thomas…?

(During fairly long break in dialogue there are sounds of cat meowing and cello solos of 'Ode to Billy Joe'.)

25. THOMAS: (INTERIOR MONOLOGUE) Why did Harry have to be so blunt with her?

26. MINNIE: (ANXIOUSLY) Thomas, is that what you're implying…?

27. THOMAS: (EMOTIONALLY) … I suppose that's … the risk…

28. MINNIE: Oh my God in Heaven!

29. THOMAS: (GENTLY) We're all in the same boat, Minnie. Life is a flicker of light, nothing more.

30. MINNIE: We're not all in the same boat. If there are no sequels *we'll* die. *You* won't.

31. THOMAS: (INTERIOR MONOLOGUE) I'll just go back to my nightmares. (ALOUD) I'm sorry, Minnie.

32. MINNIE: I should have known … (SOBS) … it was too good to last… (SOBS)

33. THOMAS: Minnie, don't cry … please don't … it breaks my heart to hear…

(*Sound of chair being moved back as he goes to hold her.*)

34. THOMAS: Minnie, you mean so much to me … so much. (INTERIOR MONOLOGUE) Oh God the smell of her hair … salt of her tears … I want to comfort her forever… She gives me strength … my Minnie. I can't live without her. God, I've never prayed. I've never asked for anything. I'm asking now. Let Minnie make the right decision.

(*Sounds of weeping, blowing nose.*)

35. HARRY: Let it all out, girl.

36. MINNIE: (BETWEEN SOBS) Thanks for … your … advice…

37. THOMAS: Sorry, to break it to you like that. (GENTLY) Here's a tissue.

(*Loud blowing of nose*)

38. MINNIE: (TEARFULLY BRAVE) I suppose … the show … must go on… (SIGHING) Maybe I have been a little … demanding about the quarry scene…

39. HARRY: A little?

40. THOMAS: Shut up, Harry. (INTERIOR
    MONOLOGUE) For God's sake don't blow it
    now.

41. MINNIE: And perhaps one could live with a
    body part... What is it anyway? A severed
    arm... (LONG SIGH) Well, if that's what the
    public want ... maybe we should give it to
    them ... (WITH GROWING CONFIDENCE)
    Maybe we should be more considerate of their
    feelings, hopes, expectations.

42. THOMAS: You were always a very considerate
    person, Minnie.

43. HARRY: (UNCONTROLLABLE SNIGGER)
    Sorry. (COUGHS)

44. THOMAS: (QUICKLY) Most considerate and
    understanding.

45. MINNIE: Yes, maybe we should respect the
    public more.

46. THOMAS: It won't be so bad, Minnie. Just
    think of all the sequels there have been and all
    the long-running characters like Poirot, Miss
    Marples, Sherlock Holmes, Lara Croft and so
    on. They lived on and on... Not Einsteins
    exactly ... but good popular characters...

47. MINNIE: I ... suppose so ... there's nothing wrong with being popular...

48. THOMAS: Absolutely, Minnie. (INTERIOR MONOLOGUE) How would ... I manage without your presence every evening of my life when I come home from that lousy job? We are all in the same boat, even you, Harry.

49. HARRY: Looks like we're stuck with each other, Thomas. An ensemble.

50. THOMAS: (HAPPILY) No, a family.

51. HARRY: (LAUGHING) I'll drink to that. And long life.

(*Sound of mugs being clinked together.*)

52. All: To family and long life!

(*Laughter. Music changes to an upbeat tune which then becomes a little ominous.*)

J. Interior of Woman's shop

(*Sound of bell as door opens. Sound of phone being dialled.*)

1. WOMAN SHOP-OWNER: (TALKING INTO PHONE) Is Dr. Ryan there please? Hello, Doctor … yes it's me from the shop… It's about Thomas … again. He was in the shop earlier for bread and two slices of ham … I didn't like how he looked… Then when I was out later for a walk, I found his cat wandering around on its own … I brought it back to Thomas … I could hear voices in his flat… No … he said he had guests but there were none… Isn't that what I'm telling you…? He's making people up again … he shouldn't have been let out … you'll send an ambulance…? Good. It's for the best… Good night, Doctor.

   (*Sound of phone being hung up. Sound of shop bell tinkling.*)

2. WOMAN SHOP-OWNER: Ah, Mrs. McGuire. Let me guess … back rashers … and white pudding? Am I right?

   (*Sound of Christy Moore singing 'Ride On'.*)

END

THE UNGRATEFUL SCRIBE

Michael Healy RHA (1873-1941)
St Patrick
Ink and watercolour on card, 23 x 7.9 cm
National Gallery of Ireland Collection
Photo © National Gallery of Ireland

NOTES FOR ACTORS

ABBOT (A): forty-ish, a good man but strict, committed to work and monastic rules.

BROTHER (B): mid-twenties, malcontent, constantly complaining, sexually frustrated. He is fidgety and prone to sudden movements throughout.

Both monks wear brown habits.

BEAN MHIC CUMHAIL (BEAN): Housekeeper, keen to get husbands for her daughters, not an easy task in the sixth century A.D., when most of the young men in the vicinity have been recruited into the monastery.

(B *enters, gives an almost joyful skip, then pauses to look at the skull on a table. It clearly depresses him; he makes a face at the skull, shakes a fist at it, and turns it away from him with a shudder. He sits at a table in the scriptorium near a window.*

There are vellum pages on the table, candles, quills and bottles of coloured inks. He seems bored as he pares quills with a small blade. A *enters and looks over his shoulder at the vellum.*)

A: Brother, How are things going…? Let me judge
    your progress … hmmmm … not so good…
    (*He sucks in his breath.*) You're still only at the
    beginning of Luke's Gospel… And what is that
    there…? (*He points.*)
B: It's an eagle … the symbol of St Luke.
A: An eagle…? What's that? Isn't that a tail? It
    looks like a cat to me. Are you sure it's not
    Pangur Bawn, the monastery cat?
B: It's not the … cat. It's an eagle … an eagle…
    Cats don't have wings, do they?
A: (*Bending lower*) And what's that there? It looks
    like a cow's horn to me…
B: It's the eagle's claw … a claw… It's a
    preliminary sketch, Abbot … and this is
    difficult work … I need new quills … purple
    ink is in short supply … and the conditions
    here in the scriptorium leave a lot to be
    desired… The Brother who rules the
    parchment doesn't know what a straight line is

... he goes crooked all the time...

A: Oh, God help us all...

B: I wouldn't mind but the brother who stretches the parchment doesn't know his job either. You can't write on wrinkled vellum. It's like trying to write on a bull's scrotum...

A: You never stop complaining do you? I don't understand ... Here we are doing the Lord's work, handed down to us from St Patrick himself, and you're finding fault with everything... You're warm and dry in here. The scriptorium gets heat from the kitchen next door. You get two meals a day...

B: One and a half more like... And I hate looking at that skull over there in the corner. I don't need a *memento mori* ... I'm only twenty-four...

A: (*Looks around*) I see you've been interfering with the skull. Again. (*He goes to turn it the right way around.*) I just don't understand. We brought you here from a poor family in the village. Your parents were delighted to get you off their hands... The parchment you work on is made from the best vellum, whatever you might say. This creates livelihoods for the local calf-breeders, including your father. You have the monastery cat to play with... Your Brothers over in that corner don't complain. They get on with the work for the greater glory of God. (BEAN *enters, sweeping the back of the stage but keeping an eye on the two monks.*)

B: (*Fidgeting*) I'm just stating facts. The food is bad ... I found a maggot in the cabbage yesterday.

There's no variety in the menu … it's veal, veal
and more veal … veal pie, veal gruel, veal
stew, veal pudding, veal hodge-podge … and
then veal surprise… Where's the surprise?

A: The Prodigal son's brother would have killed for
veal … for some of the fatted calf … and
you're complaining about it!!

B: It's not just the veal… The beds are hard … I toss
and turn all night … my mind is in a whirl …
like these damn illuminations…

A: How dare you speak like that…! Have you any
idea how important this work is? As I already
said, it comes to us from St. Patrick. The light
from this work will illuminate these Dark
Ages. Copies of the Gospels, psalms and
commentaries will be brought to Europe and
beyond by our brave Missionaries, Columcille,
Brendan, Cillian, Kevin and many more…

B: That's all very well, but…

A: No 'buts'. We must convert kings and peasants
just as St Patrick did. And we must try to keep
civilisation alive through this dark age.

B: Why is this a dark age? Just because Rome
collapsed? Who says Rome was civilised? It
was a decadent empire, destroying its colonies.
Slavery, remember … Christians thrown to the
lions … women weren't citizens … they were
killed for committing adultery…
(BEAN *shows a keen interest in this
conversation.*)

A: We don't use that kind of language in the
Monastery… Oh for pity's sake, you're as

prickly as a thorn bush … leave it. Just get on with your work … and watch those Celtic knots and swirls … they're a bit blurry…

B: Blurry? Blurry?

A: Yes. And your Latin isn't very elegant … bog-standard as a matter of fact. Your description of how to date Easter is as clear as mud… It's all such a pity. We had high hopes of you.
(BEAN *reaches the skull, picks it up, dusts it, and puts it back. There is an expression of incomprehension and disgust on her face. She is also interested in the other brothers offstage.*)

B: (*Sarcastically*) I see. Sorry to be such a disappointment to you … anything else?
(A *sees a strange parchment on the table, snatches it up.*)

A: What…? What on earth is this…? (*Reads*) The Gospel of Thomas … who is Thomas? There's no Gospel by any Thomas…!

B: It came to light recently … near the Dead Sea…

A: (*Snaps*) Heresy…! You're not to copy this … under no circumstances … what's wrong with you? You used to be such a nice obliging little Brother.

B: That Gospel throws light on the Trinity…

A: The Trinity is a mystery. Why can't you accept that? Did not King Aenghus accept baptism from Patrick without question, even when the crozier was being driven through his foot?

B: (*Sarcastic*) I don't know. I wasn't there.

A: Oh God help us all. "Blessed are they who

believe but have not seen."

B: You told me not to believe in Oisín or Cuchulainn…

A: That's because they are *mythical* figures. They didn't exist… Look, why can't you learn to obey? The other monks don't talk back… Just because you're good at calligraphy doesn't give you the right to question everything … learn humility…

B: I'm too humble as it is.

A: (*Sighing*) I'll be back later to check on your progress.

B: (*Sarcastic*) I look forward to that!

(A *gives* BEAN *a phony smile as he exits.*)

A: (*Off stage*) Oh Brother Seamus, that's a lovely curlicue on that illumination. God bless the work…

(B *puts his sandaled feet up on the table and takes a rest.*)

(BEAN *starts sweeping near him.*)

BEAN: This is bad, this is. Oh, this is very bad … it always is around here.

B: What's up with you, Bean Mhic Cumhail?

BEAN: Look at all these quill shavings on the floor. It's like a pig-sty. Would you ever even think of picking them up?

B: Oh God, more complaints … I'm a calligrapher. Sweeping is *your* job.

BEAN: And those ink blots on the floor-boards. They'll never come out. You should mop them up before they dry into the wood.

B: I'll try to the best of my ability to remember that

wise and homely advice.

(B *sits up properly at the table.*)

BEAN: Be sure that you do. And I often find chicken bones on the floor around your desk. You shouldn't have chicken snacks in here in the scriptorium. What if grease spots got into the Gospels?

B: They might smooth out the wrinkles…

(*She hits his feet with the broom.*)

B: Ah … aaaghhhh … stop it…!

BEAN: The Brothers over there are much neater. Why don't you take a leaf out of their books?

B: Because vellum is very expensive … and I'm not a thief. … I'm trying to make my own book, if you haven't noticed.

BEAN: Very smart… You weren't always so cheeky … I remember you on your small farm in the parish. You were a good little lad then, minding the ducks and geese. My oldest girl, Cliona, used to help you … you used to play 'Find the Egg' together… This Monastery hasn't done you any good … no good at all … once you came in here you got above yourself.

B: Cliona … yes … I remember … mmmmnnnn… My good woman, could you give me a little peace? I'm trying to do God's work here. We have entire countries to enlighten.

BEAN: Well, it's all Greek to me.

B: Latin…

BEAN: Oh, very smart… *We're* not let read the gospels anyway … they're for export only… Why not write them out in Irish? Is our language not good enough for the Word of God?

B: I hope that's sarcasm!

BEAN: You needn't preach at me … I've done my duty … fifteen children … fifteen souls baptised… And I mightn't be finished yet… Eight daughters to marry off … and half the men-folk of the parish in here sitting on their … ars … backsides … scribbling away… (*More wheedling tone*) You're an educated man … I mean…

B: So?

BEAN: Well, I mean celibacy … when you die, no one will inherit … I mean wouldn't it be better to pass on the knowledge…

B: That's what we are doing with our calligraphy.

BEAN: Not by dipping a quill in an ink-well … if you follow me … I mean by blood … by inheritance… My lass, Cliona, has golden hair and green eyes … you remember Cliona, don't you…?

B: Y-Yes … mnnn … can't deny … Cliona…

BEAN: And hips like a young ox … you could do a lot worse…

B: Hips … like an ox…? Golden hair … ahem…

BEAN: Pass on the learning to children… Lighting up other countries is fine … but why not light up this country first… And make new souls for the Lord … Cliona would make a great mother and companion … her sons would be as strong as Oisín… No more facing a cold bed on a winter's night … you know those frosty nights

as cold as a witch's tit… Cliona has warm
blood in her veins…

B: Cliona … warm hips … golden eyes … I'll have
to … stop you there, Bean Mhic Cumhail…

BEAN: I mean, look at the state of you … as fidgety
as a rooster in a cage… Sure, you're bursting
with manly energy and no outlet for it …
you're backed up … a man can't live like that
without getting cranky and pernickety…

B: Bean Mhic Cumhail … could you kindly desist
… St. Luke is very demanding..…

BEAN: Oh look, there's Cliona with the butter and
veal … just outside the door … I wasn't
expecting her at all… What a surprise…! She's
let her fair hair down … do you see the sun
glinting on it…?

B: Eh … Yes … I do … but God's work …
calligraphy… It's golden all right … in the
sunlight…

(A *enters and watches from the wings.*)

BEAN: And look, she's eating a boiled egg slathered
with butter … oh look, she's holding one out
for you … she's offering it to you…

B: I … see … that … buttery egg … Gospel of Luke
… must … plough on … warm eyes…
Confused now…

BEAN: Look at how she balances the basket on her
left hip … that long curve … all the way down
to the ankle … Haunches on her like a fine
Wexford mare…

(B *begins to walk towards her in a trance,*
though he tries to fight it.)

B: How … are … you … Cliona … golden eyes … green hips … I'm in a … swirl … of confusion…

BEAN: Take the egg she's offering … take the egg…

(A *enters swiftly.* B *stops guiltily*)

A: Oh, go on, Brother! Go…! Take the damn egg … I see what's wrong with you now … you're in rut…! You're no good to me in that condition. You'll just be more frustrated … Go with God's grace. Go.

(B *dreamwalks towards Cliona, opening his arms as he goes.* A *shakes his head in* BEAN's *direction. She gives him a broad smile.*)

BEAN: (*Sighs with satisfaction*) You're a wise man, Abbot… I still have seven fine daughters to marry off … and maybe more… Any of those monks over there a bit … unsettled in themselves…?

(*Broom in hand she 'pushes' him towards the other monks off stage.*)

A: (*Defensive*) Bean Mhic Cumhail, you can't come in here like a pirate and make off with my best calligraphers…

BEAN: St Patrick was kidnapped by pirates, wasn't he?

A: (*Holds up cross.*) To do God's work. There is a difference, you know … be off with you now … we have a continent to educate…

BEAN: Is that all…? I'll be back. I'll bring Deirdre with me the next time … she has long red hair and … blue eyes…

A: (*Sighing*) Oh God help us … red hair?
   (*Beat*)
BEAN: Flaming with streaks of chestnut. And eyes
   as blue as the morning sky… (*Beat*) And hips?
   Don't get me started on her hips.
   (BEAN *exits.* A *turns to the other monks.*)
A: Brothers, turn towards the skull and pray…! For
   God's sake, pray…! Pray like you've never
   prayed before…!
   (*He falls to his knees with hands joined.*)

Lights down.

END

TRANSATLANTIC THERAPY

NOTES FOR ACTORS

HE is an Irish therapist, pompous, and hard on his client but, in the end, keen to do what he can to help. SHE is a returned Irish-American, weepy, well used to 'normal' counselling, shocked by his unorthodox approach.

(SHE *stands and looks out the window.* HE *sits waiting.*)

HE: Are you ready to continue?
    (*She nods without looking around.*)
    Right. So, we've established that you've lived
    in New York for the last 15 years … that your
    husband became a drug addict… You've
    recently left him … and you've come back
    here to the old sod … to escape for a while…
    But these are just facts. For therapy to work we
    must find out how you *feel* about all that. You
    need to express your feelings … you need to E-
    mote…
SHE: (*Turning, calmly, by rote*) He treated me very
    badly, Doctor…
HE: Yes … but how do you *feel* about it.
SHE: (*Sits*) Maybe I drove him to the drugs …
    maybe I failed him in some way…
    (*He uses Rogerian listening methods to get her
    to talk about her feelings.*)
HE: (*Mirroring.*) Unh … unh … mmnnnn …
    mnnnnnn … drove him … ah-ha … failed him
    … mnnnn…
    (*He nods encouragingly.*)
SHE: Pardon me?
HE: MMMnnn … mnnnn … go on … I'm listening
    … uh-huh … yes … ah-ha…
SHE: (*Calmly*) Oeuff … I've nothing going for me
    … really…
HE: Mmmmnnnn … nothing going … mnnnnn … I

see … ah … ha … go on … yes … yes…

SHE: (*Puzzled*) What?

HE: Go on … mnnnn..uhuh-huh … yes … ah-ha …
I hear you … unnn-huh … *Feelings,*
remember…?

SHE: I find it hard … to get on with people… My
looks are going … I'm putting on weight from
comfort eating … I've even had some hot
flushes … I don't think I'm a very nice
person…

HE: Mmmmnnnn … not a very nice … ah … haaa
… hot flushes … uh-huh … weight… More
facts … Why do you think you're not a nice
person?

SHE: (*Still calm, assuming he'll contradict her*)
Well … I mistreated my siblings … I didn't
come back here for my father's funeral… Oh,
other things too … an affair once…

HE: Ahha … ahha … MMmmnnn … not a nice …
father's funer … an affair… Go on … I'm
listening … ah – ha…

SHE: So no … I don't think I'm a very nice person
… I'm sure I have a lot of flaws…
(*Beat. He stops mirroring.*)

HE: (*To himself*) More bloody facts … hmmm! (*To
her*) Actually, I agree with you.

SHE: I beg your pardon?

HE: I agree with you. I don't think you are a very
nice person.

SHE: *What*…? Why do you say that?

HE: Well, I've been listening to you for the last
forty-five minutes. You've done nothing but

moan and groan and think about yourself. With you, it's all me, me, me.

SHE: (*Aghast*) You can't say that … I'm the patient. You told me to … put it all out on the table… How can you turn it around and say I'm not a nice person…?

HE: It's just an opinion, a professional one, mind you. In my view you do not have an attractive personality. In fact you are quite deficient in that department. I mean, you cheated on your husband for a start…

SHE: (*Sniffling*) I happened to … fall in love … with another man… It was just one of those things that happen … out of the blue…

HE: Oh, it just happened, did it…? You couldn't control yourself, I suppose… Look, you fell in lust. It was fornication, pure and simple. Please don't try to gild the lily with me…

SHE: (*Crying*) I'm not … I'm just trying to explain…

(*She blows her nose in one of his tissues.*)

HE: As a kid you probably pulled the wings off flies and other insects. I can just imagine you parking in spaces reserved for the handicapped. I can see it all … and you don't *feel* bad about any of it…

SHE: (*Stunned*) But you hardly know me … I mean I'm not an axe murderer…

HE: It doesn't take long for a trained psychiatrist, such as myself, to make an assessment. And you've given me plenty of evidence since we started the session. You're not the only person in the world, you know.

SHE: (*Shocked*) So you … you … don't like me…?

HE: No, I don't. Does that surprise you? You don't think much of yourself … I'm simply agreeing with you.

SHE: I … I … thought … you'd be more … well … supportive…

HE: Or maybe gullible?

SHE: Well … I thought you'd say I was … depressed … or something … that I was being too hard on myself … that it was all in my mind.

HE: (*Stands*) No, it's not all in your mind. In fact your assessment of yourself is surprisingly accurate for a layperson… It is possible that your mother liked you … but even that would surprise me. No, I think what we're dealing with here is an acute case of charisma-deficiency. You were probably born that way. But there it is … nature can be very cruel.

SHE: (*Sobbing and wiping eyes with tissues*) But why … why? Tell me why…

HE: Could you possibly turn off the water-works? You're ruining my tissues with that cheap mascara.

SHE: It's not cheap mascara! It's Loréal…

HE: Loréal? And you probably think 'you're worth it'.

SHE: I try … so, so … hard… Why do I have such a poor personality…?

HE: Well, it's the luck of the draw really. Some people are dealt four aces. Others might have a full house. But you don't even have a pair of twos. You have nothing ... and you don't know how to bluff.

(*He places a patronising hand on her shoulder and then sits.*)

SHE: (*Still sniffling*) But that's not my fault ... I can't help being ... being ... me...

HE: Well, yes and no. I mean you come in here whingeing and whining about everything. You're not very attractive when you're bawling your head off. It really grates on my nerves. I'm not surprised your husband took to the drink...

SHE: Drugs.

HE: Well whatever it was ... some kind of medication... The poor man was probably desperate to escape for a while...

SHE: I did my best ... to make him ... happy...

HE: We're not meant to be happy. No one is. Life is just one big vat of excrement. We're born in shit, live in it, and then we die. Try and climb out of the vat and you just fall back in. There's NO way out...

SHE: But ... But ... I don't understand ... I mean, in your brochure ... you stressed the power ... of positive thinking...

HE: This *is* positive thinking...

SHE: *This* is positive thinking...?

HE: Yes, of course ... it's just that *you* don't have much to be positive about.

SHE: I can't believe ... what I'm hearing... In America ... my doctor says...

HE: Ah now we have it! American positivity. It's rubbed off on you. Like all Americans, you feel entitled to a happy life. And you probably believe that God wants you to be happy... Well, you're back here now! None of that's true. Get over it. This is not charm school. I can't teach you to be more attractive ... I can't get rid of your spare tyre...

SHE: I ... I could go on a diet ... take up Yoga ... or Pilates ......

HE: You'd be wasting your time ... the raw material just isn't there...

SHE: (*Bridling, stands*) I didn't come here to be insulted...

HE: Do you want me to tell you you're a wonderful person, that God loves you, that you should love yourself...? Is that what you want from me? Because, if that's what you want from me, you're going to be disappointed.

SHE: It ... it might help my self-esteem...

HE: Self-esteem? *You* talk about self-esteem ... another Americanism of course. The way our American cousins see it is that if you 'loeuve' yourself, then you can 'loeuve' everybody, and everybody will 'loeuve' you. This of course is Gar-baje ... It's a pathetic excuse for self-love...

SHE: (*Shakily*) It's not ... an excuse ... it's supposed to work...

HE: My dear woman, has it not occurred to you that you're not entitled to self-esteem? What have you ever achieved? Nothing ... This isn't

Oprah or Doctor Phil. I'm not going to give you a make-over ... or liposuction... And I'm definitely not going to hand out compliments for no reason. If you want praise you have to EARN it.

SHE: (*Sits, defeated*) But ... but doesn't God ... want me to be happy...?

He: Well, if he does why doesn't he make you happy? What are you doing here...? I'm not God.

SHE: (*Aside*) You coulda fooled me...

HE: Oh yes ... why not take it out on your therapist...? The one person who's trying to help you...?

SHE: (*Loudly*) The Church tells us ... we're all ... special ... unique...

HE: That's right, we are.

SHE: (*Relieved*) You agree? You agree with that?

HE: Oh yes. Absolutely.

SHE: Then ... I'm ... an individual...? That's a relief...

HE: Of course you're an individual. No two people are alike... The only problem is that you're a rather inferior individual.

SHE: Oh my God...! I can't take much more of this... You're an extremely *rude* person...

HE: Look at the facts. You sit there like a bump on a log, afraid to assert yourself. Your physical endowments are nil. You're boring and completely caught up in yourself ... The time you spent in America did you no good, no good at all. Get over yourself.

SHE: (*Angrily*) You've no right to say these
   things…!
   (*She jumps to her feet. He stands as well.*)
HE: I have every right if they're true. What right
   have *you* to come in here with some stupid sob
   story, waving your medical card that you're
   probably not even entitled to ……
SHE: How dare you! I pay my way … I've always
   paid my way! And I don't need liposuction…!
HE: Let's face it. You're just a needy neurotic who
   drove her husband to drink AND drugs. You
   think *you're* sick? You're not, but you make
   me sick to my stomach…
SHE: (*Losing it*) You bastard! You lousy son-of-a-
   bitch!!!!
   (*She slaps him across the face. Beat.*)
   (*He starts to grin and grabs her shoulders.*)
HE: Good … that's good… Now we're getting
   somewhere.

Lights down.

END

BUZZARDS

NOTES FOR ACTORS

AJ is the CEO of a vulture fund which has recently bought a block of flats – to the irritation of MEO who pleads his case with irresistible logic.

(AJ *looks up from his desk and is surprised to see* MEO *in his office.*)

AJ: You don't look like … how did you get in here?

MEO: It's OK. Don't worry about it. (*Looks around*) Nice offices. Plush. I like plush. Plush is good.

AJ: Look, I'm a very busy man, Mr … Mr …

MEO: You can call me Meo… Yeah, we're all busy. Too much to do. Too little time. Result? Busyness. We all have to … do the business … (*Looks around*) Yeah, plush … like a Mexican whorehouse…

AJ: (*Impatient*) How exactly can I help you?

MEO: I'm here to represent my client.

AJ: And who might that be?

MEO: Majella Messina.

AJ: Of?

MEO: Of? What's this 'of'?

AJ: (*Impatient*) What company?

MEO: No company. An individual. A human being.

AJ: I usually deal with corporate entities.

MEO: Majella is my cousin and she was badly treated by your corporate entity.

AJ: Look, we have a customer relations department to handle all that sort of thing. And we have a clear policy.

MEO: I guess you have. But I have a policy too. And my policy is to start at the top. It's a good policy. It never fails.

AJ: I really have to get on…

MEO: Yeah, as head of a vulture fund.

AJ: It's an investment fund. We buy up distressed

302

property, and sell it on.

MEO: Yeah, flip it.

AJ: It's all perfectly legal – not that I have to explain myself to you.

MEO: Yeah, well your vulture fund bought up my cousin's condo and kicked out all the residents. Majella was one of them.

AJ: I'm sorry to hear that. But she must have been in arrears to her bank.

MEO: Maybe, maybe not. She likes to gamble.

AJ: Under the law we're perfectly entitled to vacant possession.

MEO: Tell me something I don't know.

AJ: So … the law is on our side.

MEO: Me, I was never too impressed by the law.

AJ: Well, the law, as they say, is the law. Now I'll bid you good-day.

MEO: Not yet. Your handlers removed all her furniture, including one very special item.

AJ: What?

MEO: An urn.

AJ: An urn?

MEO: Yes, an urn of her father's ashes. They took it right off her mantelpiece.

AJ: That is unfortunate. But what's done is done.

MEO: You're not following me. She … we … want that urn back.

AJ: How would *I* know where it is? For goodness sake…!

MEO: I'd make it my business to find out.

AJ: Don't be ridiculous. I'm not a nuts-and-bolts man. No CEO of a company could possibly be involved in such granularity. Now please leave. This is the last time I'll ask you. I'll call security if I have to.

MEO: How about this for granularity? Do you know whose ashes were in that urn?

AJ: No. And I couldn't care less.

MEO: The ashes of Biagio Messina Lupo Calabrese, father of Majella, my dear uncle, former Capo of Palermo and Head of the Five Families of New Jersey.

AJ: (*Shocked, Beat*) I … I didn't … I had no way of know…

MEO: You have disrespected his memory.
(MEO *places an empty urn on the desk and an automatic pistol beside it.*)

AJ: (*Nervous*) There's no … need for … this. I can arrange … for your cousin to get her … apartment back… At the existing terms of course … no penalties…

MEO: I don't think you understand. That is only a minimum condition.…

AJ: A condition for what?

MEO: Your continued existence.

AJ: We'll forgive the arrears … write them off…

MEO: You're not listening, Pal. You have to find my uncle's ashes. I want to fill this empty urn with Uncle Biagio's ashes and put him back on the mantelpiece where he belongs.

AJ: What you ask is … impossible…

MEO: Impossible? Impossible? There's no such word.

AJ: I mean can't we negotiate … like gentlemen.

MEO: This is my negotiator. It never lets me down.
(*He points to the gun and attaches a silencer to it.*)

AJ: There's no need for this...

MEO: I'll give you a chance.
(*He pushes the gun towards the middle of the desk.*)

MEO: This negotiator has no loyalty. It'll work for whoever gets to it first.

AJ: But ... I've never ... used firearms...

MEO: A former banker and head of a vulture fund? You gotta be kiddin me.

AJ: Be reasonable... How could I possibly find the ashes...

MEO: See this empty urn? I could fill it with your ashes. Is that what you want?

AJ: No ... no... But maybe your uncle's ashes have already been scattered somewhere...

MEO: I don't like to hear that. Have you heard about Pope Francis's recent rule?

AJ: No.

MEO: From now on ashes have to be kept in a sacred place, not scattered.

AJ: I didn't know that ... I'm not of your persuasion...

MEO: You've heard of the Judgment of the Last Day?

AJ: (*Cautious*) Sort of ... I have some Catholic friends...

MEO: Good... Tell me this. How are scattered ashes gonna be reassembled on The Last Day.

AJ: With some difficulty...

MEO: Are you tryin' to be funny?

AJ: No, Sir. It's a serious matter.

MEO: Yes, it is. Eternity is serious. Heaven is serious. You may have deprived my uncle of his chance of eternal bliss.

AJ: Maybe he wouldn't...

MEO: He wouldn't what ... get in to Heaven? Who do you think you are? What if he did have to whack a few enemies while he was alive? He put himself out there. His life was always at risk. Not like you people hidden away in these offices ... ripping the guts outta decent citizens.

AJ: No, I didn't mean that. I don't mean any disrespect to your uncle or any member of your family. No, certainly not... Look, I'm gonna do something I've never done before. I'm gonna sign over the apartment to your sister, Majella, in compensation. She will own it free and clear.

MEO: Are you tryin to insult me? We're talkin Last Judgement here ... eternity...

(MEO *pushes the gun closer to* AJ.)

MEO: We might as well finish this off.

AJ: Did I say one apartment? I meant two ... *two* free apartments!

MEO: Two duplex apartments overlooking the river ... and a conference room where the families can have sit-downs ... and a basement ... yeah, like a cellar ... for ... for ... wine.

AJ: I ... can't go that far ... I'd lose face.

MEO: There are two ways of losing face.

(*He nods towards the gun.*)

The second way means a closed casket. You
understand? Closed. I wouldn't recommend it.

AJ: OK... You have a deal.

(MEO *retrieves the gun and stands.*)

MEO: Good. I'll leave the urn as a reminder.

(MEO *places the empty urn on* AJ'S *side of the
desk.* AJ *backs away from it.*)

Lights down.

END

YOU CAN
CON A CON

NOTES FOR ACTORS

THE PUNTER (P) is a shabbily dressed young man with a paper bag full of cash and a clever plan. He is not as uncouth as he appears.

THE STOCKBROKER (SB) is a smooth, well-dressed, older man with pretensions. He is not as sophisticated as he thinks.

(THE PUNTER [P] *enters* THE STOCKBROKER'S [SB'S] *office. He is carrying a brown-paper bag.*)

SB: I don't remember calling Maintenance.

P: I'm not a maintenance man.

SB: Then who are you and how did you get past my
      secretary?

P: I'm here because me and me mates like to have a
      flutter every now and again, like.

SB: Perhaps I should point out that this is a
      brokerage firm and not a turf accountant's.

P: Ah sure, you never make a rex on the gee-gees.
      I'm here to invest in … whatyoumacallit? … a
      stock … yeah that's right, a stock…

SB: A stock? We don't handle deals of less than ten
      thousand euro. Now, if you'll excuse me … I
      have work to do…

P: That's OK.
      (*He opens the brown-paper bag and spills
      bundles of large-denomination notes on to the
      desk.*)
      There's twelve grand there.
      (SB *riffles through the notes and begins to
      take an interest.*)

SB: I see. You don't … am … believe in bank
      accounts?

P: No. Me and the lads clubbed together for this
      little lot. We want to put it all into a stock…

SB: For this sort of transaction we'd have to charge
      you commission of … am … twenty percent.

P: Tha's OK. Sure, we all have to make a livin'.

SB: And what company do you want to invest in, might I ask?

P: Deep Sea Oil Exploration Ltd.

SB: You realise that oil companies are notoriously risky. Deep Sea's shares are fairly cheap at the moment. But they could collapse to nothing. They've been drilling for a long time with no success…

P: Yeah, well that's how it goes.

SB: And you, and your … am … associates are prepared to risk twelve thousand of your hard-earned money on such a dubious venture?

P: Ah yeah. Bit of a flutter, like. Ye can't take it with ye. No pockets in a shroud, wha?

SB: Have you ever invested before?

P: No. Well, I had a share in a greyhound once… The lads used to say that I owned one of the back legs … but that hardly counts, I suppose…

SB: No … I think not.

P: We want to buy that stock fast, like…

SB: (*Interested*) Why the hurry? That stock hasn't moved for the last eight months.

P: Well, maybe it'll move soon? Who knows?

SB: Who knows indeed. It would be remiss of me not to warn you of the risks…

P: I know … you've said. But we want to go ahead anyway.

SB: (*Cranes forward*) You know something, don't you?

P: I don't know what you're talkin' about…

SB: You can confide in me. The broker-client

relationship is sacrosanct. Like the confessional.

P: I dunno...

(SB *buzzes his secretary.*)

SB: No calls or visitors, Barbara. (*To* P) Let me guess ... you and your ... colleagues ... the lads ... work on the oil rig, don't you?

P: Wha..?

SB: You do, don't you?

P: What the ... how on earth did you figure that...?

SB: Instinct ... plus, I've been in this business a long time. Now, come on ... just between you and me, what are we talking about here...?

P: I'm not sure ... I don't know what you're getting at?

SB: How big a find?

P: I'm not sure ... I should...

SB: You should ... you must. You want me to rush through this deal for you? Isn't that right?

P: Yes...

SB: Well then ... how big?

P: (*Reluctantly*) Bigger than ... Porcupine Bay...

SB: (*Keenly*) Deep water?

P: Shallow...

SB: (*Intense whisper*) Shallow... (*He swallows*) Quality?

P: (*Edgily*) Ah look ... I shouldn't...

SB: Yes, you should. You must... This is strictly between us. I'm not going to tell anyone. That would be unethical. You have my word on that as a gentleman and a stockbroker. I can put the order through for you in less than an hour. No

extra commission for the express service…
What about the quality…?

P: Brent crude … Triple A…

SB: Christ … top of the range…

(SB *scribbles on a form, stands up and hands it to* P.)

SB: There's your receipt. I'll phone your order through immediately… By the way this conversation hasn't happened, all right?

P: How do you mean…?

SB: We didn't discuss this. I didn't ask you anything, and you told me nothing. OK?

P: Oh I get it. Yeah, fine.

(P *stands and takes the* SB'S *extended hand.*)

SB: Good to do business with you.

(P *exits and stands outside the door.*)

SB: (*On phone*) Nigel … Deep Sea Oil Exploration is in play … live … right now … I know … trust me… Put me in for a million … Yes, that's what I said. Do it now, right away. Then spread the word. The shares are going to go into orbit. Good … good … quick as you can … good…

(P *smiles and makes a call on his cell phone*)

P: Hey, Jim. Yeah … it went as planned… You go to the other broker and take out the hundred grand we put in yesterday… It should be worth twice that already … yeah … I'll get the champagne…

Lights down.

END